MW01286951

"Nothing has supported
resonate deeply with th
Scripture as a Disciple of Je.... .. you are looking to jump-start, refresh, or
deepen your followership of Jesus, this book is a great place to start."
Todd Hunter, author of *What Jesus Intended*

"Throughout the ages, Christ-followers have affirmed the astonishing
good news that we can encounter the living God as we read the Scriptures.
In his careful reflections on the way that Dallas Willard read, taught, and
lived the Scriptures, Dave Ripper guides us step by step into how we can
open our hearts and minds to this divine encounter. This accessible book
deepened my desire to live more deeply with one foot in the Bible and
my other foot in my everyday life. I believe it will also do this for you."
Trevor Hudson, author of *Seeking God* and *In Search of God's Will*

"*Experiencing Scripture as a Disciple of Jesus* should be central to every
church's disciple-making plan and taught to all Jesus followers. Many are
stuck in their spiritual journeys due to reading the Bible like any other
book, rather than as one seeking an encounter with God. Dave Ripper
expands on Willard's principles, making them accessible to those committed to growing more like Jesus and desiring the peace, joy, and contentment he promises. This approach is essential for anyone seeking a rich
and vibrant spiritual life. Following Dave's methods will transform us
through our encounter with the living God."
Charles Galda, president of Vision New England

"In *Experiencing Scripture as a Disciple of Jesus,* Dave Ripper maps out the
clues left by Dallas Willard for engaging with the Bible. Through story
and scholarship, Dave weaves a comprehensive invitation for meeting
God up close and personal through Scripture. Read this book, accept the
helpful invitations at the end of each chapter, and prepare to get to know
Jesus more deeply than you did before."
Lacy Finn Borgo, spiritual director and author of *Faith Like a Child*

"Dallas Willard has had a remarkable impact on an inordinate portion of
the church. In this book, Dave Ripper helps guide us through how to not
only read but also be shaped by the Scriptures that contain unique power
to illumine the human condition."
John Ortberg, founder of BecomeNew.com

"*Experiencing Scripture as a Disciple of Jesus* offers Dave Ripper's insightful sharing of Dallas Willard's soul-filled passion for Scripture and spiritual practices. Willard desires humanity to daily experience eternal living. Ripper discusses Willard's mindset theologically, philosophically, experientially, reflectively, transformationally, lovingly, unhurriedly, and mystically. Willard desires Christ-followers to encounter an intimate 'with-God life' experience, soaking in God's Holy Book. Embracing God's Word and disciplines provide paradigms for deep and spiritual immersion."

Barbara L. Peacock, Dallas Willard Award winner and founder of Peacock Soul Care

"I've often wondered how Dallas Willard arrived at such fresh takes on familiar Scriptures. After reading *Experiencing Scripture as a Disciple of Jesus,* I understand—and better yet, Dave Ripper's practical exercises will help me do it for myself."

Ted Harro, president of Renovaré

"It's refreshing to find a book that's authored by a pastor who believes Christlike formation is the central mission of the local church and has discovered ways to place the Scriptures in the middle of an authentic spiritual, formational experience. Pastor Dave Ripper loves and lives Dallas Willard's approach and invites us to do likewise as healthy disciples of Jesus."

Stephen A. Macchia, founder and president of Leadership Transformations Inc. and author *Broken and Whole*

"Dave Ripper knows and loves the Scriptures, and he knows and loves Dallas Willard. With the heart of a pastor, the insight of a biblical scholar, and the skill of a biographer, Dave becomes the channel through which his love and knowledge are forged by the grace and power of the Spirit into this truly remarkable offering for apprentices of Jesus. I sense Dallas smiling over this book and saying, with a wink to Dave, 'You got it!'"

Howard Baker, professor emeritus of spiritual formation at Denver Seminary and author of *The One True Thing*

"Through years of study, practice, and learning, Dave Ripper has synthesized the ideas of Dallas Willard and applied them to his life and ministry. Dave shares his personal journey and includes his method of interacting with Scripture to aid our moving from communication to communion with God."

Bill and Kristi Gaultiere, cofounders of Soul Shepherding and authors of *Journey of the Soul*

"In this clear and compelling book, Dave Ripper provides an illuminating treatment of how Dallas Willard's experiential approach to reading Scripture can enrich the spiritual lives of everyday followers of Jesus. The book includes a must-read chapter for ministry leaders interested in a way of preaching and teaching that deepens their own and others' spiritual formation. Highly recommended!"

E. Trey Clark, assistant professor of preaching and spiritual formation and dean of chapel at Fuller Theological Seminary

"In *Experiencing Scripture as a Disciple of Jesus*, Dave Ripper has offered a beautiful gift to both the global church and the spiritual formation movement. Many pastors quote Dallas Willard's ideas, but few have successfully implemented them into the culture of their church. This book makes the compelling case that integrating Willard's vision for spiritual formation in the church begins with understanding his experiential approach to encountering God through Scripture. As an experienced pastor and longtime student of Willard, Ripper draws on his deep grasp of Willard's thinking to inspire fresh wisdom, practices, and methods for seeding his insights into our own souls and local church communities."

Brandon Shields, director of church formation at Practicing the Way

"Three kinds of people are going to benefit richly from Dave Ripper's new work. The first group? Men and women who preach from the Bible regularly. They'll find themselves reaching for this book frequently—both as a source and for illustrative ideas—to bring their sermons to life. A second group? Leaders of small groups looking for dialogue on the nature of Christian living. And a third, much larger group? People of diverse ages and stations of life (like me) who are looking for the kind of personal inspiration that keeps one's spiritual journey alive and well. I particularly loved Ripper's powerful Dallas Willard insights about a life strengthened and guided by the regular reading of the Bible."

Gordon MacDonald, pastor and author of *Ordering Your Private World*

"Dallas Willard's life and writings have deeply influenced many of us. *Experiencing Scripture as a Disciple of Jesus* helped me remember that one of Dallas's greatest gifts to me was his unique approach to the Bible. Dave Ripper helped me see how Dallas invited us to rediscover the beauty of God's written Word engaged in communion with the living Word. This book was a profound gift to me."

Alan Fadling, author of *A Non-Anxious Life*

"Reading *Experiencing Scripture as a Disciple of Jesus* unlocked something deep within. It was as if the Scriptures weren't just inspired but inspiring me to new depths with my rabbi. This book is chock-full of thoughtful, wise, and deeply practical stories that make Dallas Willard's study methods accessible to us all."

Steve Carter, lead pastor of Christ Church of Oak Brook and author of *Grieve, Breathe, Receive*

Experiencing Scripture as a Disciple of Jesus

Understanding

Through the Spirit

Apprenticing

(*Reading the Bible like Dallas Willard*)

Dave Ripper

Foreword by Gary W. Moon

An imprint of InterVarsity Press
Downers Grove, Illinois

InterVarsity Press
P.O. Box 1400 | Downers Grove, IL 60515-1426
ivpress.com | email@ivpress.com

©2025 by David Scott Ripper

InterVarsity Press® is the publishing division of InterVarsity Christian Fellowship/USA®. For more information, visit intervarsity.org.

Scripture quotations, unless otherwise noted, are from the New Revised Standard Version, Updated Edition. Copyright © 2021 National Council of Churches of Christ in the United States of America. Used by permission. All rights reserved worldwide.

Scripture quotations marked MSG are taken from The Message, copyright © 1993, 2002, 2018 by Eugene H. Peterson. Used by permission of NavPress. All rights reserved. Represented by Tyndale House Publishers.

While any stories in this book are true, some names and identifying information may have been changed to protect the privacy of individuals.

Photo on page 15, in the introduction, was taken by the author and reproduced by permission of the Willard Family Trust. Image may not be reproduced in any form without written permission.

Quotes from Dallas Willard's teaching recorded on audio and video and "My Prayer for You" on page 16 are used with permission of Dallas Willard Publications, dwillard.org. Permissions for use of Dallas Willard's work that has been previously published in print must be obtained directly from the publishers.

The publisher cannot verify the accuracy or functionality of website URLs used in this book beyond the date of publication.

Cover design: Faceout Studio, Spencer Fuller
Interior design: Jeanna Wiggins

ISBN 978-1-5140-1310-6 (print) | ISBN 978-1-5140-1311-3 (digital)

Printed in the United States of America ♾

Library of Congress Cataloging-in-Publication Data
A catalog record for this book is available from the Library of Congress.

32 31 30 29 28 27 26 25 | 12 11 10 9 8 7 6 5 4 3 2 1

For Dallas Ripper

in honor of Dallas and Jane Willard

Contents

Foreword

Gary W. Moon

SINCE YOU HAVE THIS BOOK IN YOUR HANDS, I'm assuming
you know about the remarkable life of Dallas Willard. So let me
ask you a question. Are you surprised that there seems to be
even more wind behind the sails of this man's ideas now than
at the time of his death, twelve years ago?

I hate to admit it, but I am at least a little surprised.

Don't get me wrong; from the time I finished reading the first
few pages of *The Spirit of the Disciplines*, back in 1988, I knew
that he, as one friend put it, is from a "different time zone" than
the rest of us.[1] He was offering a special gift for the body of
Christ that would need to be slowly unwrapped and savored.
Before finishing that book, I had already begun searching for
excuses to be in the same room with Dallas. And since that time,
I have devoted much of my vocational and avocational life to
telling folks about his soul-shaping ideas.

Eventually, and to my great good fortune, this fixation on
Dallas's teaching led to my being asked to be the founding director of the Martin Institute and Dallas Willard Research
Center at Westmont College. And to my joyful surprise, I was
presented the opportunity to write his biography. Even so, and

after declaring him to be a notable reformer who was making life-giving contributions to the church on par with Ignatius of Loyola, Martin Luther, Teresa of Avila, and John Wesley, I still have to admit that I'm a little surprised that the gales of interest behind this man's contributions seem to be picking up speed.

Let me now offer a few brief reflections on three *why* questions: Why the surprise? Why is this movement still growing? Why is the book in your hands so important?

Why the surprise? Dallas Willard was a professional philosopher who became more widely known for his speaking and writing as an "amateur" theologian. So I have wondered if he would be accepted by those in the guild of professional theology. Also, his true north goals were so lofty as to seem audacious to some. To inspire and equip pastors to become "the teachers of the nations"?[2] I remember trying to talk him out of those words for a conference theme. I failed. To see "spiritual formation become part of the domain of public knowledge"[3]? Really?

Dallas was not shy about swimming against the current of a very long and treacherous river of resistance in pursuit of the good. Down deep, I wondered if others would be willing to step into the stream and invest the energy it would take to keep swimming against the current, toward such distant goals.

Why is this movement still happening? Well, for starters, the man just keeps publishing. I remember, while in the process of writing the biography, books using his words from recorded talks kept being published. At one point, years after Dallas died, I said to a friend, "If he doesn't stop writing, I'll never be able to finish." But fortunately, the flow of his recorded and published ideas did not stop and continues to be heard and read across a variety of channels.

I also think that, as Dallas so often reminded listeners, his concepts were not new or trendy. And that is true. His great genius was seeing the synthesis in the ideas and experiences of the great devotion masters through the centuries. Dallas kept his focus on the golden thread of encounter with divine presence that runs through the tapestry of experiential theology, not on denominational distinctives. Dallas knew that Jesus is still making disciples the same way he was two thousand years ago: by walking right up to a student and saying, "Hello, what is it that you really want?" and "Follow me."

The movement is also still happening because so many of the older voices and ministries that have been influenced by Dallas Willard continue to grow and are becoming stronger. But more importantly, there is a growing stream of younger voices emerging in a variety of vocations: skilled communicators and influencers, such as John Mark Comer and Jon Bailey; philosophers like Steve Porter, Rebecca DeYoung, and Brandon Rickabaugh; theologians like Michael Stewart Robb and Keas Keasler; skilled teachers like Carolyn Arends; and law school professors and social justice advocates like Brandon Paradise; to name only a few. And with the publication of this book, we can add to the list pastors such as Dave Ripper.

Why is this book important? I read the manuscript *Experiencing Scripture as a Disciple of Jesus* with great excitement and anticipation. My lofty hopes were exceeded. You will quickly discover that Dave has invested the time—almost two decades— to get the importance of his mentor's appreciation for Scripture. You will also discover that he has the heart of a pastor and the pen of a storytelling teacher.

Yes, there is a model to follow, a well-designed approach for reading the Bible as Dallas would and did. But if you look closely, you discover at the heart of the plan a simple yet profound idea. If you want to read the Bible like Dallas, you have to believe you have a reading partner; the apprentice-making rabbi who will step right off the page and say hello. A relationship maestro who wants to engage you in conversation and create opportunities for communion as you walk together on a pathway that leads into the life and heart of God.

The sofa where Dallas Willard sat each morning for long periods of Scripture reading has a permanent indentation where he sat by a lamp. I'm sure there would be a second such mark next to his seat, if his rabbi and reading partner had not been sitting so lightly on the blue fabric. That's how Dallas read and experienced his Bible. He used two lamps.

So if you want to walk along the pathway that leads into union with the Trinity, as you read Scripture like Dallas did, Dave's book offers lamplights to make that pathway more clear and visible.

Introduction

Encountering Dallas Willard

*We should also make every effort to sit regularly under the
ministry of gifted teachers who can lead us into the Word and
make us increasingly capable of fruitful study on our own.*

DALLAS WILLARD, *THE SPIRIT OF THE DISCIPLINES*

WHEN DID YOU FIRST ENCOUNTER the name Dallas Willard?
Chances are you're holding this book because at some point
along your spiritual journey, his words, his ideas, or maybe even
Dallas himself left an indelible impression on you or someone
you know. Meeting Dallas has led countless Christians to *re-
think their thinking*, as he liked to say, about the possibility of an
eternal kind of life with God—not just later, but now.[1] He had
a remarkable way of saying what many of us suspected or hoped
to be true about Christianity, but struggled to put into words.
Dallas lived and died as a luminary—pointing the way toward
the availability of the kingdom of God among us.

I first came across the name Dallas Willard at the Westminster Abbey bookstore in London in 2005. It was my junior
year of college, and I was taking a course called Revisiting the
Reformation, taught by two religion faculty members at Grove

City College. Our two-week trip through Europe began in England and finished in Germany. While the history of Anglicanism was fascinating to study on location, I felt something was missing as I listened to hours of lectures on the life and work of Thomas Cranmer and his fellow English Reformers. My mind was overflowing with information, but my heart was yearning for something more.

While perusing Westminster Abbey's bookstore as we waited to depart for our next stop on the study tour, a peach-colored book appeared to leap off the shelves, arresting my attention. It was titled *Devotional Classics*, edited by Richard Foster and James Bryan Smith. I recognized Foster's name, and so decided to leaf through the book. I quickly discovered this work was a compilation of what Foster and Smith deemed to be the most important writings throughout Christian history on the spiritual life. A fitting topic for what my heart longed for.

I immediately recognized the first entry: C. S. Lewis and an excerpt from *Mere Christianity*. Following Lewis, the next selection was a piece from someone named Dallas Willard, on the topic of the of the cost of *nondiscipleship*.[2] *What a gripping turn of phrase,* I thought.

While I had never heard of this man who taught philosophy at USC for decades, I thought he had a really awesome-sounding name. Within a few paragraphs of reading his vision for discipleship, I became enthralled by his thought. "The word 'disciple' is used 269 times in the New Testament," he wrote. But the word *Christian* he said, "is found only three times and was first introduced to refer precisely to disciples. . . . The New Testament is a book about disciples, by disciples, and for disciples of Jesus Christ."[3]

Who reads the Bible like this? I wondered. In all the New Testament classes I had taken, I had never come across an observation that seemed to strike so closely to the heart of what these twenty-seven books are about.

This insight mattered so much to me because at that time all the rage in pastoral training seemed to be solely about the ABCs of church growth: attendance, buildings, cash. *The better you are as a pastor, the bigger your church will be*—that was the underlying assumption then (and probably is still all too prevalent today). Yet Willard, like a voice crying out in the wilderness, prophetically called the church back to its original mission: discipleship. I had never heard anything like this. Quickly I realized, I want what this guy Dallas Willard has found.

As our bus boarded, and as I heard someone yelling "C'mon, Ripper!" I hurried to scrounge together the eleven pounds needed to purchase the book and make it back before the doors closed and the bus departed. In this case, I'm glad to have only learned later that Dallas insisted, "You must ruthlessly eliminate hurry from your life."[4]

As I reflect on this basement bookstore experience twenty years later, it's not an overstatement to say that moment changed my life forever. No, it was not the history, not the grandeur, not the royal traditions of Westminster Abbey—or even the Reformational theology I learned on the trip. It was the discovery of a name, a person who God used to birth a passion within me personally and pastorally for Christian spiritual formation. Meeting Dallas helped me meet God like never before.

TWO LANDSCAPES

Through nearly two decades of reading, studying, and even getting to know Dallas personally as a student in one of his classes, I've observed an essential feature of his life and teaching: he endeavored to "live at the cross section of two landscapes."[5] A visible realm and an invisible realm. A physical world and a spiritual world. We must "get used to . . . looking at things you cannot see," Willard would insist—taking his cue from Paul's words in 2 Corinthians 4:18.[6] To live in only one of these two landscapes—the physical or visible world—is to miss life's greatest opportunity: experiencing the kingdom among us now as Jesus' disciple.

Not only do I find myself struggling to live at the cross section of the visible and invisible realms, but as a pastor, I also find myself attempting to live across the expanse of two other worlds God has called me to inhabit: the local church and the spiritual formation movement. For those not familiar with the term *spiritual formation*, in *Renovation of the Heart*, Dallas Willard states that distinctly Christian spiritual formation "refers to the Spirit-driven process of forming the inner world of the human self in such a way that it becomes like the inner being of Christ himself."[7] This, according to Willard, is fundamentally what the work of discipleship is all about.

While the spiritual formation movement finds its origins in the life and ministry of Jesus—and certainly even earlier in the Old Testament eras—its current resurgence dates back to the 1970s. James Bryan Smith, the Dallas Willard Chair of Christian Spiritual Formation at Friends University, writes, "As a young man, I was privileged to be an eyewitness to the rise of the Christian spiritual formation movement. It began its modern form, in 1978, when Richard Foster wrote what has become the perennially standard text on the spiritual disciplines, *Celebration of Discipline*."[8] Within a decade of the release of this seminal work (which was influenced by Willard's Sunday school classes that Foster participated in), thousands of people who had hardly taken spiritual disciplines seriously before—disciplines like solitude and silence, service and study—were now practicing them regularly.

Given the widespread desire for focused teaching on the spiritual disciplines of the Christian life, Foster launched a new ministry called Renovaré (Latin for "to renew"), one of the first of dozens—perhaps even hundreds—of ministries and nonprofits committed to the work of spiritual formation worldwide.

This makes me wonder: Why do so many organizations like these exist? While I'm thankful for the great formational work done by many in these ministries, I believe so many exist because the local church—by and large—has failed to live out its primary calling of helping people become conformed to the image of Christ and to do everything Jesus said (see Gal 4:19; Rom 8:29; Mt 28:19-20). While you would naturally assume spiritual formation would be the central work and aim of the local church, it is sadly far from it.

To close the gap between the visible and the invisible, Willard wrote adamantly and repeatedly that the local church must make its mission to be *a center for spiritual formation*.[9] This charge is one of the reasons many pastors and ministry leaders like me have found the writings and teachings of Dallas Willard so alluring.

But while thousands of pastors have been drawn to what Willard has said and often quote what Willard wrote, few have enacted his compelling vision within the context of the local church. Spiritual formation remains incidental to the mission of the church rather than integral to it—even among those of us who treasure Willard's works. How might this change?

Before answering this question, let me first make a confession to all the pastors and ministry leaders reading: integrating spiritual formation into the life of a local church is hard! While I want to drive this essential initiative forward within my own context, plenty of things always seem to interfere. Pastoral needs arise, emails stack up, crises occur. Sunday keeps coming! Amid everything it takes to continue doing what seems indispensable to the work of the local church—worship services, preaching, life-stage ministries, pastoral care, outreach—it's hard to imagine how to do even more. Where is there room for what looks like the *added* work of spiritual formation?

Consider this with me for a moment: What if spiritual formation wasn't meant to be an *addition* to your work in church, but was the *mission* of your church? Let me state this declaratively: spiritual formation was not meant to be in addition to the work of the church, because spiritual formation *is* the mission of the church.[10]

To bridge the gap between the spiritual formation movement and the local church, I'm convinced a key aspect of Dallas Willard's thought deserves fuller attention and implementation: his approach to reading, teaching, and living the words of Scripture. If local evangelical churches are largely anchored by the words of Scripture in their preaching, programming, and outreach, then shaping how churches approach Scripture is essential.

This book's focus is to present Willard's experiential approach to reading Scripture theologically, biblically, practically, and accessibly, in hope that local churches may become centers for spiritual formation. Reading Scripture like Dallas Willard will not only help close the gap between the work of local churches and spiritual formation organizations, but will help followers of Jesus—like you and me—live at the glorious cross section of the visible and spiritual worlds.

THE PATH AHEAD

Over the past decade, I've been privileged to have opportunities to talk about Dallas Willard's vision of spiritual formation at conferences, retreats, churches, and in academic settings. At the conclusion to my presentations, there's often a time for questions. Surprisingly, the question I seem to be asked most is: "Dave, if you could ask Dallas Willard anything, what would you ask him?"

Over the years I've typically responded by noting how Dallas said he operated under the assumption that he was wrong about a few things. I'd ask him what he thought he might be wrong about. More recently, though, my answer has shifted. Just as Jesus' disciples asked Jesus to teach them to pray (Lk 10), I would ask Dallas to teach me to read the Bible like he did. While I wish I had asked Dallas this question *directly* when I had the chance, I'm grateful that I've discovered, in the years since studying with him, what I believe he would have taught me.

In what follows, I will present how I've learned to read Scripture more like Dallas did. While he never devoted an entire book to reading the Bible, his theology of Scripture, methodology for studying it, and personal practices of Bible engagement can be found scattered throughout his lectures and the five primary books he wrote, which have been referred to as the Willardian corpus: *Hearing God, The Spirit of the Disciplines, The Divine Conspiracy, Renovation of the Heart,* and *Knowing Christ Today.*

I developed this content over the course of my doctoral program through Fuller Theological Seminary and the Martin Institute and Dallas Willard Research Center at Westmont College, under the advisement of Willard's biographer and friend, Gary W. Moon. It's the culmination of my efforts to weave together what Willard has said about reading Scripture throughout the body of his work, in hopes that this important aspect of his thought could become more widely known, accessed, and applied. *My vision*: to demonstrate how encountering God through Scripture is a primary vehicle of authentic Christian spiritual formation. *My desire*: for you to experience the Bible as a disciple of Jesus so that you will become and live more like Christ.

In chapter one, I share why we should read Scripture like Dallas did. I introduce you to his experiential approach to interpreting and teaching the Bible. If you've ever been awed by one of Willard's interpretations of Scripture but wondered how he arrived at such a conclusion, this chapter provides an avenue to help you interpret Dallas Willard's biblical interpretations.

Chapter two examines how Willard read the Bible with the reverence of a Southern Baptist, the intellect of a philosopher, and the heart of a mystic. These categories help explain why Willard's interpretations are so resonant to his readers yet so unlike what is ordinarily found in evangelical biblical commentaries. We will discover that Willard advocated for what he called *biblical realism*. Inviting you to read the Bible realistically is one of my central purposes for this book.

Building on these categories, chapter three uncovers how Willard read the Bible *transformationally*—not merely *informationally*. While much of what Willard wrote appears new to his readers, Willard believed he merely recovered what has been lost or forgotten throughout Christian history. Given this, chapter four focuses on how Willard's approach to reading Scripture has striking parallels to the work of Ignatius of Loyola. In chapter five, I attempt to assimilate all that has been taught into a practical and memorable way of reading Scripture, following the manner of Dallas Willard. The pattern I developed is called the IMMERSE method. This acronym stands for Immersion, Meditation, Memorization, Encounter, Response, Supplication, and Experience.

Chapters six and seven explore specific ways Willard read the Old and New Testaments respectively. Finally, chapter eight outlines how pastors, ministry leaders, and Bible teachers can learn from the unique way Dallas Willard taught Scripture and apply it to their own contexts.

At the end of each chapter are experiential exercises for personal reflection, spiritual practice, and group conversation. Following the conclusion, an appendix summarizes twenty key principles for reading Scripture like Dallas Willard.

As a preacher, I often ask myself as I prepare a sermon: (1) What do I want them to *know*? (2) What do I want them to *do*? (3) What do I want them to *feel*? Throughout this book, there's a lot that I want you to *know*—to renew the mind biblically, theologically, spiritually. There's also a lot that I hope you will *do*—to put into practice Willard's Bible-reading approach. *Apprehension* comes through *application*. But there's also much I desire for you to *feel*.

As you read this book, I pray you have the sense that a renowned teacher and Christ-follower like Dallas Willard has invited you to go on retreat with him to learn how to experience the Bible as a fellow disciple of Jesus. Sometimes you'll hear Willard speak professorially from the lectern. Most often, though, you'll hear Dallas's loving voice in conversation over a shared meal as he gently draws your attention toward the presence of God. Know that I count it a privilege to be on retreat with you as together we imagine what it might be like to learn to read Scripture like Dallas did.

THE BIBLE DALLAS READ

In June 2023, following my graduation from Fuller in Pasadena, California, I brought my family to the Willard home in Chatsworth, California, so I could introduce my wife and kids to Dallas's lovely wife, Jane. Specifically, I wanted her to get a chance to meet my oldest son, Dallas, who—not shockingly—was named after her late husband. (Despite the Cowboys, it really is an awesome name. But this is coming from a Pittsburgh Steelers fan.) Their home felt like a thin place, as the Celtic Christians would say—an ordinary place that seemed a step or two closer to heaven.

As part of Jane's generous hospitality, she let me peruse the personal Bible of Dallas Willard. Willard's NASB Bible had a cloth cover to keep its contents intact. Tape supported the binding and held together many of its delicate pages. The Bible was still bookmarked—perhaps to signify where Dallas had last left off before he died in 2013—at John 15. For a person who lived such a *with-God life*, as he called it, it was only fitting that his Bible was bookmarked at Jesus' grand invitation to abide with him.

What made this Bible unlike any other Bible I have ever seen, though, was that virtually every chapter of every page of it was

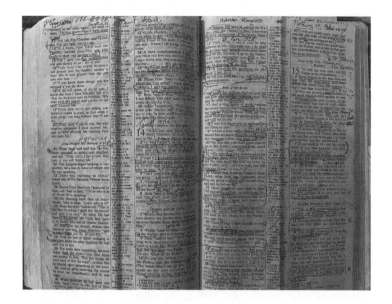

filled with underlined phrases, circled words, highlighted verses, and handwritten notes that arguably only Dallas could have understood. (Jane was unsure about the significance of the various ways Dallas marked his Bible.) The margins of each page were imprinted with impressions made from Dallas's hands during the long hours he spent studying, memorizing, and being with the Father, Son, and Holy Spirit through these ancient, living words.

As I ran my fingers along the tattered edges of Dallas's Bible, I thanked God for the sacred privilege it was to hold my earthly hero's most treasured text. Initially I thought, *One day I hope my Bible will look like this.* But then I hoped for more: *May I encounter the author of the Bible like Dallas did, when he sat down to read God's Word.*

The experience of looking at, reading, and even praying the words of Dallas's Bible reminded me of what I had long thought about through the research of my doctoral dissertation. *Scripture itself is like a thin place,* an invitation to live at the cross section of two landscapes with God. The Bible is a gateway to eternal living.

WILLARD'S PRAYER FOR YOU

As you go on this journey of reading Scripture like Dallas Willard, know that I am praying for you, the reader. I hope that you will share moments with God like I did at Westminster Abbey's bookstore, as I discovered the unique and powerful way Dallas read the Word of God. As a blessing over you, I'd like to offer this prayer from Dallas—a prayer he extended to his many students and readers. In the summer of 2013, it was printed as a bookmark that was shared with those who attended his funeral.

My Prayer for You

That you would have a rich life of joy and power, abundant in supernatural results, with a constant, clear vision of never-ending life in God's World before you, and of the everlasting significance of your work day by day. A radiant life and a radiant death.[11]

1

Scripture as a Gateway to Eternal Living

*We cannot have a relationship with the
Bible, but the God of the Bible.*

DALLAS WILLARD, *HEARING GOD*

*I SHOULD HAVE TAKEN my high school typing class far more
seriously.*

I thought this about a hundred times as I furiously tried to
capture everything Dallas Willard said throughout the weeklong
class I took with him in 2010 through Denver Seminary.[1] The
course was held at The Hideaway Inn and Conference Center
in Colorado Springs, in the shadow of what has been called
America's Mountain, Pikes Peak. It was a fitting setting to meet
and study under the person who has become the most towering
spiritual influence in my life.

In the conference room at The Hideaway, I learned the essential *message* of Dallas Willard through his profound lectures.
While he is often and generally associated with the spiritual
disciplines, the scope of his teaching extended greatly beyond
this. During our time together, through the use of an old-school

transparency projector—a Willard staple—he helped us discover a picture of the gospel Jesus preached. He enabled us to understand what the kingdom of God is really about and its availability here and now. Eventually, he made his way toward the spiritual disciplines and concluded the course by casting a vision for the local church to become a "school for eternal living"—whatever that meant.

He finished his formal teaching with the most freeing words I ever heard as a young pastor: "What God gets out of your life is the person you become." What God gets out of my life is not my success as a pastor or the size of my ministry. The person I become matters most. That *is* good news.

Never before or since have I come across a person whose teaching carried so much weight. Every sentence he uttered spoke volumes. Every idea he introduced possessed authority. Every pause pulsated with spiritual power.

Like most students of Dallas Willard, I wasn't able to come close to understanding all the revolutionary things he said in real time, so I resolved to capture as much as I possibly could for later reflection. Fifteen years later, these are some of the takeaways from Dallas's teachings that I've come to treasure most from my notes:

Joy is "a pervasive sense of well-being."[2] It's possible for you to be okay even if everything around you isn't.

Beauty is goodness made sensibly present.[3]

Does the gospel I preach have a natural tendency to produce disciples or only consumers of religious goods and services?

If you want to do everything Jesus said, don't *try* to do everything he said. Instead, *train* yourself to become the kind of person who would "easily and routinely" do everything he said.[4]

While I learned the *message* of Dallas Willard in the conference room, what left an even greater impression on my life was interacting with the *man* in all the other spaces of The Hideaway. For a person who was once described as "a man from another 'time zone,'" Dallas was surprisingly down-to-earth.[5]

He was funny. When talking to my wife, Erin, and me over a meal, he described how he met his wife, Jane, at his college's library. "I checked her out, but I never checked her back in."

He was normal. One evening, Dallas watched the college football national championship game with us—even though USC wasn't playing. Other retreat leaders I had interacted with over the years were almost impossible to connect with outside of the formal sessions. It was a relief and a joy to discover that this philosopher seemed more at home hanging out as our friend than alone as a monk.

He was helpful. Dallas slowly and patiently guided me through some of the confusion I had around spiritual practices and theology. For instance, I posed a "hypothetical" situation to him.

"Dallas, if you're fasting and your wife cooks you dinner, what do you do? After all, Jesus tells us to fast 'in secret.'"

"Dave, if you're fasting and your wife cooks you dinner, you eat. The point of the spiritual disciplines is not to get good at them, as much as they are designed to help you love God and love others more fully. The more loving thing to do is to eat what your wife has prepared." It wasn't the answer I was looking for in the presence of my wife, but I'm confident it was the right answer!

And yet Dallas was devout. As the only married couple in the class, my wife and I ended up staying in a suite that shared a wall with the room Dallas was in. Every morning we awoke to the sound of Dallas's baritone voice singing hymns as part of his morning time with the Lord. Our class followed Dallas's spiritual practice of fasting on Wednesdays along with him. Somehow being with the man—experiencing his personal presence and his personal spiritual practices—seemed to confirm his message, adding even more gravity to his groundbreaking thought.

Since that course, I spent years first trying to learn *what* Dallas said about the topics he addressed—especially his unique interpretations of many passages of Scripture. In more recent years, though, as part of my doctoral studies, I have sought to discover *how* Dallas reached the conclusions he did.

I have been grateful to learn that others have pursued similar ends. In his outstanding academic work *The Kingdom Among Us: The Gospel According to Dallas Willard*, Michael Stewart Robb shares his email correspondence with Willard, regarding how he arrived at many of the biblical and theological conclusions he came to hold—viewpoints that do not seem to fit squarely in any one Christian tradition. In response to Robb, Willard writes:

> Nearly all of my "influences" are from people long dead. I have arrived at my views by studying the Bible philosophically, if you wish, and by reading widely through the ages, and trying to put it all into practice. It is presumptuous to say, but I believe that God has guided my thinking. Certainly nothing I have is really new or "my own."[6]

In the next chapter, I will attempt to explain the basics of the philosophical terms and approaches that characterized

Willard's work, like *robust metaphysical realism, epistemic realism*, and *phenomenology*. Before then, though, I'd like to use more accessible language to explore how Willard read the Bible philosophically. To do so, we must first build a foundational theological understanding of Willard's view about the nature of God and what the gospel is. To rightly perceive what the Bible is, we must know the God who lovingly gave it to us. Second, I'll present a case study of the text Willard arguably quoted the most through his teaching and writing, John 17:3. By building this foundation, we will be prepared to craft the core framework for how Willard read Scripture like a Southern Baptist, a philosopher, and mystic.

WHAT COMES TO MIND WHEN DALLAS THINKS ABOUT GOD

In *The Divine Conspiracy*, Willard writes that when we think about God, we should conclude that he leads a very interesting life, and that he is pervaded with joy. In fact, he believes God is the "most joyous being in the universe."[7] Because he is abundantly loving and abundantly generous, God is infinitely joyous. What an astonishing way to think about God!

To illustrate this enthralling vision of the nature of God, Willard describes an overwhelming experience of beauty he had off the coast of South Africa. It occurred to him that God sees brilliant scenes of wonder like this all the time. Willard reflects, "It is perhaps strange to say, but suddenly I was extremely happy for God."[8] To deepen his reflections even more, Willard posits, "But he [God] is simply one great inexhaustible and eternal experience of all that is good and true and beautiful and right."[9] This is what we should think of when we think of God's perfect being—God's very life. And this life—his life—is the life God desires to share with each one of us.

God desires to share his joyous life with us because, as 1 John states, God is love (4:8, 16). Woven throughout the tapestry of Willard's works is his belief that the essential nature of God is love.[10] Later in *The Divine Conspiracy*, Willard concludes, "The acid test for any theology is this: Is the God presented one that can be loved, heart, soul, mind, and strength? If the thoughtful, honest answer is 'Not really,' then we need to look elsewhere or deeper."[11] Given God's loving nature, his people are invited to live what Willard described as the *with-God life*, which is central to his understanding of the gospel.

THE GOSPEL OF THE KINGDOM

To grasp Willard's understanding of what the Bible is and how it is to be read and applied, we must examine Willard's subversive perspective on what the gospel is. In *The Divine Conspiracy*, Willard claims that the Christian message proclaimed today is focused only on how to deal with sin, or what he calls "gospels of sin management." When surveying the broad spectrum of Christian belief and practice, he observes that the right side of the theological spectrum focuses almost exclusively on the forgiveness of an individual's sins. On the left end of the spectrum, the gospel is viewed as a removal of social or structural evils.[12]

Given these shortsighted understandings of the gospel, Willard believes Christians devolve into being people who are merely ready to face the judgment of God at death, or those who are committed to pursuing love and justice in society.[13] In our politically and religiously polarized world today, it is apparent that these distinctions Dallas Willard wrote about in 1997 are just as true today—perhaps even more so.

While Willard contrasts the differences between right and left gospel perspectives, he also draws comparisons to what they have in common. Neither group, he believes, provides a "coherent framework of knowledge and practical direction adequate to personal transformation toward the abundance and obedience emphasized in the New Testament, with a corresponding redemption of ordinary life."[14] The gospels of sin management simply do not offer a clear path to a life of apprenticeship to Jesus.[15]

My background and tradition were largely bent toward the right side of this gospel continuum. Presentations of the gospel I heard were almost exclusively about death, and not life. Related to this, the Reformational theology I was taught in college bordered on making "the atonement the whole story," as Willard warns against doing. To shed light on this common perspective in evangelical circles, Willard asserts, "justification has taken the place of regeneration, or new life. Being let off the divine hook replaces possessing a divine life 'from above.'"[16] In contrast to atonement as the whole gospel, Willard offers a gospel for living—life to the full here and now (Jn 10:10).

According to Willard, the gospel is "the good news of the presence and availability of life in the kingdom, now and forever, through reliance on Jesus the Anointed." Crucial to this definition is the reliance on the *person* of Jesus and not simply the *work* of Jesus. We are called to trust Jesus—the real person—to experience the good news of the gospel, rather than merely "trusting some arrangement for sin-remission set up through him—trusting him only as a guilt remover." Trusting Jesus as a person means we have confidence in him for every aspect of our lives. Trusting Jesus means we believe that he is right about everything and sufficient for all that we need.[17] Trusting Jesus is what enables people to experience and enter into an eternal kind of life now. Building off his understanding of the gospel, Willard clarifies what he believes the Bible teaches about eternal life.

JOHN 17:3 CASE STUDY

According to Willard, the only definition we have of eternal life in the Scriptures comes from John 17:3, in which Jesus says, "This is eternal life, that they [his disciples] may know you, the only real God, and Jesus the anointed, whom you have sent."[18] While it can be tempting for people—especially those with gospel leanings toward the right end of the spectrum—to interpret knowing Jesus as mere "head knowledge" or mental assent, Willard argues that *to know* in the Bible "always refers to an intimate, personal, interactive relationship."[19] Thus he concludes, "The eternal life of which Jesus speaks is not knowledge about God but an intimately interactive relationship with him."[20] Do you see what this means? We do not have to wait until we die to experience eternal life. Rather, as we *know* God, we can experience *eternal living* today.

This understanding of the gospel and knowing Jesus is paramount for reading Scripture like Dallas Willard. We are not to approach the Scriptures to merely know what is true, but to know the one who says, "I am the way and the truth and the life" (Jn 14:6). We are to read Scripture in a way that invites communion with the trinitarian God of love, the one who is the most joyous being in the universe.

While Willard's interpretation of John 17:3 and its implications are inspiring and resonate, he does not explicitly show his readers each of the steps he took to reach this interpretation. To better understand how Willard drew this interpretive conclusion, let's consider the different ways one can know something, which Dallas would have had in mind. These are best summarized through the words of one of his PhD students, philosopher J. P. Moreland, in Moreland's tribute to his professor and friend.

According to Moreland, there are three essential forms of knowledge: propositional knowledge (true belief based on adequate grounds); know-how (wisdom, skill); and knowledge by acquaintance (direct experience).[21] To expound on these ideas, propositional knowledge "is knowledge that an entire proposition is true"; in other words, it is justified true belief.[22] *Know-how* is the ability or capacity to do certain things. It is characteristic of the knowledge of a skilled practitioner. Moreover, it is the "ability to engage in the correct behavioral movements, say by following the steps in a manual, with little or no knowledge of why one is performing these movements."[23] *Knowledge by acquaintance* is when we are directly aware of something. According to Moreland, it is sometimes called simple seeing or direct experience of something or someone.[24] Perhaps an illustration will help clarify and distinguish these three forms of knowing.

At a church where I previously served, I have a good friend named Ted. Ted has brewed coffee for many different ministries and events at the church for the past two decades. He possesses an incredible, almost encyclopedic knowledge of all things coffee: its composition, consistency, and origins. Ted is well educated in the physical impact coffee has on the different types of people who drink it. He has a robust understanding of the economics of the entire coffee business. This understanding of coffee that Ted possesses is what we have described as propositional knowledge.

Not only does Ted know a lot about coffee; he knows how to roast it and brew it in a variety of styles—from drip to cold brew to French pressed. His capacity to roast and brew coffee is know-how. But while Ted's know-how and propositional knowledge of coffee are seemingly as bottomless as a refillable mug at a diner, Ted does not actually drink coffee. In fact, he will often ask others how it tastes. Ted possesses propositional knowledge of coffee and know-how for roasting and brewing coffee, but he does not have what we have described as knowledge by acquaintance. To really know coffee, you have to actually drink it. The tasting of coffee is the direct, firsthand, experiential way of knowing coffee.

I believe this understanding of knowledge by acquaintance is what guided Willard to interpret John 17:3 the way he did. And it's a driving factor in how Willard read all of the Bible. The good news of the gospel according to Dallas Willard is that, through the words of Scripture, you can possess more than just propositional knowledge of who God is and what he's done. Hearers of the Word can gain more than just simple know-how for living life well and wisely. The Bible invites us to experience knowledge by acquaintance—relational knowledge—with the relationship that is at the center of the universe: our triune, loving God. You can know Jesus by acquaintance—directly, personally, interactively. You can experience a transforming friendship with Jesus that begins now and lasts forever as you apprentice your life to his. Jesus' invitation to everyone is to taste and see and experience life in the kingdom. Scripture is a gateway to eternal living.

Before moving on, it is important to highlight an additional principle Moreland raises about knowledge, which coheres with Willard's views. Moreland adamantly believes knowledge does not require certainty. He contends, "If knowledge is just a sort of certainty, then knowledge 'with certainty' would be redundant."[25] What this means for spiritual knowledge is that when we seek to know God or understand certain biblical texts, we should not assume that our search requires reaching a state of total certainty, free of all doubt. While Moreland is not stating that certainty is a bad thing, he is noting it is not required to have genuine knowledge. In the spiritual life, we are pursuing confidence, not certainty. In our cultural moment of deconstruction, maintaining the distinction between certainty and confidence is vital for readers and teachers of Scripture. Much of the confidence we discover through knowledge by acquaintance with God and the Scriptures could be described by Willard as being *self-authenticating*.[26] In other words, we gain confidence in our knowledge of God and his ways as we obey his teachings and experience God and his Word as real.

KNOWING DALLAS BY ACQUAINTANCE

Prior to the 2010 class I took with Dallas, I had acquired propositional knowledge about his thought through the books and articles of his I read. I also possessed know-how for teaching and quoting Dallas to add depth and authority to my preaching and teaching. But after gaining personal, interactive, experiential knowledge of Dallas, I knew him by acquaintance.

Prior to having this experiential knowledge of Dallas the *man,* I only possessed knowledge of Dallas's *message.* Knowledge of his message convinced me that he absolutely had something to say—a message I must take seriously and pay attention to. But after getting to know Dallas personally, I became convinced his message was right. My experience of Dallas living what he taught proved the veracity of what he said. My experiential knowledge of Dallas fueled my commitment to not just knowing what he said or understanding why he said what he did. Meeting Dallas convinced me that I could live more fully into the kingdom of God than I was. I could experience a deeper, eternal kind of life here and now.

I share this not to sing the praises of Willard, but to illustrate the fuller, richer, more intimate way we may know God through the Scriptures. We do not need to settle for mere propositional knowledge of God or the core doctrines of the faith—as essential as these are. Neither do we need to be content in simply knowing how to apply certain truths from Scripture to our lives. We can know God with a knowledge by acquaintance, which lies at the heart of the gospel for today. As we open the pages of the Bible, we are invited to experience eternal living now as Jesus' apprentices. The good news of the Bible is that we can know its author.

EXPERIENTIAL EXERCISES

1. John 17:3 was one of the biblical passages Willard referenced most. Spend time memorizing and meditating on this verse.

2. Based on John 17:3, this chapter stated that "Scripture is a gateway to eternal living." Have you ever had experiences

of reading Scripture when you encountered the presence of God in a personal way? If so, reflect on what that experience was like. Can you recall what parts of Scripture you read when you were able to know God more directly, personally, or intimately?

3. Read passages of Scripture where the word *know* is used in a prominent way. Examples include: Psalm 46:10; Psalm 139:1; Philippians 3:10-11. As you read the word *know* in these passages, read in light of what was described as *knowledge by acquaintance*. How does this shape your understanding and experience of these texts?

4. Pray the words of Ephesians 1:17-19. Ask God that you might know him in an ever-deepening experiential way.

I pray that the God of our Lord Jesus Christ, the Father of glory, may give you a spirit of wisdom and revelation as you come to know him, so that, with the eyes of your heart enlightened, you may perceive what is the hope to which he has called you, what are the riches of his glorious inheritance among the saints, and what is the immeasurable greatness of his power for us who believe, according to the working of his great power.

2

Southern Baptist, Philosopher, Mystic

*Dallas Willard's life experiences provided this Southern Baptist
minister, professional philosopher, amateur theologian and
practical mystic with an appreciation and approach to Scripture
that was most unusual. He was able to simultaneously maintain
a high view and deep love of the Bible—as evidenced by the wear
on the cover and the notes scribbled in every margin—while being
able to view it in a way that was outside most Christian boxes.*

GARY W. MOON, *ETERNAL LIVING*

HOW DO YOU READ THE BIBLE?

One way we may begin to answer this question centers on
intent. You read the Bible for the purpose of devotion, or prayer,
or study. If you're a preacher like me, you may read the Bible
because Sunday's coming, and sermons must be prepared. Or to
be more real, perhaps you often read Scripture simply because
it's what a good Christian is supposed to do. In other words, you
read to assuage any guilt you might feel for *not* reading the Bible.

Another approach to answering this question focuses on
methodology—how we go about reading the text. Maybe you

read Scripture by following a pattern like the *REAP method* (read, examine, apply, pray). Alternatively, you might follow a more intense inductive method of studying the Bible, or you might experiment with the ancient approach of reading Scripture known as *lectio divina*, or sacred reading. Its fourfold progression begins with reading (*lectio*), continues to reflecting (*meditatio*), moves toward responding (*oratio*), and concludes with resting (*contemplatio*).[1]

Let's consider this question—*How do you read the Bible?*—from one other angle. What are the influences and the people whose voices have shaped the way you read the Bible the way you do? Did you learn to read Scripture from a particular theological tradition or Christian organization like InterVarsity Christian Fellowship or Cru, or from a youth leader, mentor, or pastor? Maybe it's been a podcast or video from The Bible Project. Take a moment to deeply consider: how and why do you read the Bible the way you do?

HOW I LEARNED TO READ THE BIBLE

I began following Jesus seriously as a freshman in high school. My faith was shaped by the two churches that were in closest proximity to my house in Western Pennsylvania, a Presbyterian USA congregation and an Italian Pentecostal church. They were only blocks away from one another, but worlds apart in style and theology. Yet somehow, both were like home to me.

At the Presbyterian church, I grew up as a young child learning the stories of Scripture, following the church calendar, and hearing the Bible read in a liturgical way. The Bible was a historical reference point that taught me *about* God and how to be a moral person. I revered this book, even appreciated it at times, but rarely read it for myself or let it shape my day-to-day life. This was my experience with the Bible until high school.

During the summer before my freshman year, I was taking my dog for a walk when something radically unexpected happened. A car full of five attractive high school girls pulled to the side of the road to talk to me. Either they wanted to pet my golden retriever or, as with Stephen in Acts 6, they thought my face was "like the face of an angel." I've gone through life choosing to believe it was the latter.

But rather than getting asked out by one of the girls, they instead invited me to come to the youth group at the Italian Pentecostal church just up the street. I'm not Italian. I didn't know what a Pentecostal was. But this was *not* an opportunity I was going to miss. "I'll see you next Wednesday," I said. Six months later, my insecure self finally worked up the courage to go.

In this church tradition, it became clear to me that there was more to Christianity than just knowing *about* God. I learned that I could know God *personally* and experientially through prayer and Scripture. Like many of the students in this growing group, Bible reading became essential to my life and formation. I paid attention to how the Holy Spirit might draw specific words or phrases to my heart. I didn't always understand what I was reading, but the possibility that God might uniquely speak to me through the pages of Scripture kept me glued to the text. The Bible became far more than a history of moral living; it was a dynamic book, inviting me to encounter the presence of God in the pages of his Word.

While my approach to reading Scripture continued to evolve and mature throughout college and seminary, my Sunday

mornings at the Presbyterian church and my Wednesday eve-
nings at the Italian Pentecostal church youth group created the
central lens through which I have read the Bible these past
twenty-five years. For many seasons, though, I struggled with
the tension created by how these two different Christian traditions approached Scripture. What brought me freedom within
this perceived tension was learning how Eugene Peterson described himself as a "presbycostal" in his memoir *The Pastor*.[2]
Rather than attempting to resolve the theological differences
between his Montana-based Pentecostal upbringing and his
Presbyterian pastorate in suburban Baltimore, he simply embraced them. While he became Presbyterian, he never stopped
being Pentecostal. One tradition did not need to supplant
the other.

Like Peterson, as my faith has matured, I've learned to
cherish the treasures I've discovered in these different traditions,
rather than being overly consumed by the troubles I can recognize in either of them. I read Scripture "presbycostally." Consider the influences that have shaped your faith journey. How
do *you* read Scripture?

Just as the variety of Christian traditions I encountered
shaped how I approach reading Scripture and following Jesus,
a similar examination of influences can explain how Willard
approached the Bible in an unusual, yet orthodox, way. According to Gary W. Moon, Willard "was able to approach
Scripture with the reverence of a Southern Baptist, the mind of
a respected philosopher and the vision of a mystic."[3] Let's consider how these facets of Dallas's life shaped his experiential
approach to Scripture reading.

READING AS A SOUTHERN BAPTIST

In 1956, Dallas Willard was ordained as a Southern Baptist minister—an ordination he maintained throughout his life.[4] Yet, to distinguish his theology and spirituality from the mainstream Southern Baptist Convention, Willard quipped that he was "a King James Baptist with a Quaker twist."[5] This "twist" perhaps accounts for how Willard maintained a high view of the authority and inspiration of Scripture like a Southern Baptist, but with nuanced understandings of key terms like *inerrancy* and *infallibility*. Willard's theology of Scripture is most explicitly stated in his books *Hearing God*, *The Divine Conspiracy*, and *The Allure of Gentleness*. We'll explore each of these texts individually to best discover how he read Scripture like a Word-centered Southern Baptist.

Willard's views and approaches to reading Scripture are most thoroughly outlined in *Hearing God*, originally published as *In Search of Guidance*. In this work, he writes,

> The Bible is *one* of the results of God's speaking. It is the *unique* written Word of God. It is inerrant in its original form and infallible in all of its forms for the purpose of guiding us into a life-saving relationship with God in his kingdom.[6]

While this initial description of the Bible's inerrancy and infallibility appears to resonate with conventional evangelical understandings of the authority of Scripture, Willard adds clarification to what he means by these two words.

First, Willard says the Bible is infallible "precisely because God never leaves it alone."[7] Second, when speaking of inerrancy, Willard believes, "The inerrancy of the original texts is rendered effective for the purposes of redemption only as that text, through its present-day derivatives, is constantly held within the eternal living Word."[8] In other words, the trustworthiness of a given text is not due to its written record we have in various Bible translations alone, but the texts of Scripture can be fully relied on in concert with Jesus, the eternal living Word.

Willard expounds on this by saying, "Inerrancy by itself is not a sufficient theory of biblical inspiration, because as everyone knows, the Bible in our hand is not the original text. Inerrancy of the originals also does not guarantee sane and sound, much less error-free, interpretations." The power and authority of Scripture, then, must not depend simply on the written word of Scripture. Rather, Willard says, "Our dependence as we read the Bible today must be on God, who now speaks to us in conjunction with it and with our best efforts to understand it."[9] These nuanced understandings of infallibility and inerrancy give context to Willard's clear and bold statements about what the Bible is and what it is not.

Dallas Willard believes that "*while the Bible is the written Word of God, the word of God is not simply the Bible.* The way we know that this is so is, above all, by *paying attention to what the Bible says.*" For instance, while the Bible is the Word of God in its unique *written* form, it is not, as John 1 makes clear, Jesus Christ, who is the *living* Word. The Bible is not the word of God that is settled eternally in the heavens (Ps 119:89). The Bible is not the word of God expressing itself in the natural world (Ps 19:1-4). Furthermore, the Bible is not the word of God in Acts that expanded and multiplied (Acts 12:24), nor is it the word sown as Jesus describes in Matthew 13. All of these, Willard says, are God's words, "as is also his speaking that we hear when we *individually* hear God."[10] Thus while the Bible is the infallible written Word of God, the word of God is not limited to just the Bible.

Willard claims, "If we try to dignify the Bible by saying false things about it—by simply *equating* the word of God with it—we do not dignify it. Instead we betray its content by denying what it says itself about the nature of the word of God."[11] Willard thus highly esteems the Bible but is cautious to ensure we do not believe things about the Bible that the Bible does not believe about itself.

Willard summarizes his theology of Scripture in this way: "The Bible is a finite, written record of the saving truth spoken by the infinite, living God, and it reliably fixes the boundaries of everything he will ever say to humankind. It fixes those boundaries *in principle*, though it does not provide the detailed communications that God may have with individual believers today."[12] This means that while God can and does speak individually to people whom he pursues union with, anything he says to his people will align within the boundaries established through his written Word.

In *Hearing God*, Willard unapologetically states that God speaks today. He's convinced there is no foundation in Scripture to suggest that God would not speak to people today through his still, small voice, or dreams and visions, or an audible voice, or even through a divine messenger or angel.[13] The Bible irrefutably demarcates the boundaries within which God will communicate, but it does not exclude God from speaking to us directly, beyond the pages of the written text.

To help clarify this tension between the written words of Scripture and our subjective experiences with God, Gary W.

Moon employs the illustration of a kite with a string. Imagine that our experiences with God are like a kite, "darting through the air, twisting and turning, driving and soaring with every breeze; the wind wants to pull the kite away, the string wants to tether it to the ground."[14] If the kite represents our experiences with God, then Scripture is the string that tethers it to the ground. For beautiful, yet controlled flight to take place, there needs to be the tension created by both the kite and string. For us to grow in our knowledge of God, we need both Scripture and individual experience with God.

Beyond *Hearing God*, Willard addresses his assumptions about the Bible in *The Divine Conspiracy*. In its introduction, Willard states, "On its human side, I assume that it [the Bible] was produced and preserved by competent human beings who were at least as intelligent and devout as we are today." Willard adds that he assumes "they were quite capable of accurately interpreting their own experience and of objectively presenting what they heard and experienced in the language of their historical community."[15]

To complement this, he speaks to the Bible's divine inspiration. He writes, "On the divine side, I assume that God has been willing and competent to arrange for the Bible, including its record of Jesus, to emerge and be preserved in ways that will secure his purposes for it among human beings worldwide." For everyday readers of the Bible, he then adds these words of hopeful assurance: "I assume that he [God] did not and *would* not leave his message to humankind in a form that can only be understood by a handful of late-twentieth-century professional scholars, who cannot even agree among themselves on the theories that they assume to determine what the message is." Given these beliefs, Willard instructs his hearers that since the Bible's purpose is practical, not academic, it should be read in an intelligent, careful, intensive, and straightforward way. This is the type of Scripture reading that is necessary for the Bible to accomplish its purpose of directing people into life in God's kingdom.[16]

In addition to these written records of Willard's theology of Scripture, his Sunday evening church class on Christian apologetics includes more of his essential reflections. These teachings were transcribed and published in the posthumously released book *The Allure of Gentleness*. Here Willard addresses central concerns related to the authority of Scripture. While some of this content overlaps with what is stated above, I have chosen to include selections from *The Allure of Gentleness* because they provide a greater sense of the tone Willard employs when responding to direct questions about the Bible.

One of the key questions Willard addresses is, "Is Scripture perfect?" He answers, "My belief is that as God gave the Scriptures, in their original form, they were absolutely perfect."[17] While he believes the originals are inerrant, Willard is not aware of any scholars who contend that our current translations of the Bible are also inerrant. But to this he adds,

> I believe the originals were inerrant, because I think that is the way God would have done it, but neither I nor any other living person has seen the originals, and frankly I'm rather glad we don't have them. Imagine what it would be like for some particular people to be in possession of them and what shenanigans would then follow![18]

Later in the section, Willard revisits this theme by suggesting that God has not preserved the originals because we would be extremely tempted to worship them instead of God himself.[19]

In an effort to summarize his beliefs about the reliability of Scripture, Willard states,

> Scripture is a reliable, historical record of events in which Scripture itself is testified to as the book of God. This is not the circular logic of people who say, "We know the Bible is true because it says it is." Instead, we say we know the Bible is true, because the standard of historiography authenticated it.[20]

To illustrate this point, Willard likens the issue of the reliability of Scripture to that of the resurrection. He surmises that "most of those who *approach it* [the resurrection] *in doubt* but remain *merely faithful to the details* find themselves believing, because the details contain such overwhelming evidence. If you approach it in that way, you don't get caught in a circle; you have the testimony of a historically reliable record."[21] From these statements we can conclude that Willard strongly believes in the historical reliability of the Bible and its inerrancy in its original form.

Beyond these crucial statements related to Willard's view of the Bible, in *The Allure of Gentleness* he urges readers to remember: "*To be a biblical Christian* is not to have high views about the Bible. *It is to seek and know and live the life that is depicted in the Bible.*" Beyond this, he warns, "One of the things that people do with Scriptures is to twist them. But notice that this is 'to their own destruction.' The Bible can kill you."[22] He suggests that, to handle the Bible wisely and reverently, when you come to the Scriptures, you should say, "Beyond the sacred page I seek Thee, Lord."[23] Thus he concludes that "anyone who approaches the Bible *for the purpose of finding God* will indeed find him and will be spoken to by God through the Scriptures."[24] For Willard, knowing the Bible is a means to the greater end of knowing God interactively and experientially.

READING AS A PHILOSOPHER

In 1965, Dallas Willard began his illustrious forty-seven-year teaching career in the philosophy department at the University of Southern California. During this time, Willard supervised thirty-one students who earned their PhDs in philosophy under his guidance. One of those students, prolific scholar and writer J. P. Moreland, reflects that Dallas was not only his professor and friend, but was like a father to him.[25] A few months before Willard's passing in 2013, Moreland spent a day with Dallas, in which Dallas expressed what his four overarching concerns were related to the future health of Christianity and the spiritual formation movement in particular.[26] These concerns perhaps best express how Willard's philosophy shaped his approach to spiritual formation and reading Scripture.

Willard's first main concern is what he describes as *robust metaphysical realism*.[27] The meaning behind this idea is that the invisible world is real, and this reality—ultimate reality—is God and his kingdom. In other words, the "physical sense-perceptible world is not all there is."[28]

Earlier I described how Dallas believed 2 Corinthians 4:16-18 teaches us that we live at the cross section of two landscapes: a visible world and an invisible world, a physical world and a spiritual world. Robust metaphysical realism is philosophical terminology for this reality. Inherent in this view is that we as human beings do not socially construct reality, such as gender.[29] There is a vast unseen world and spiritual reality—namely God and his kingdom—which provides the source of moral knowledge. Truth, then, is not something we create from our own experiences and perceptions of reality. Rather, ultimate reality is discovered through God's revelation. The concern of robust metaphysical realism is the focus of Willard's *The Divine Conspiracy: Rediscovering Our Hidden Life with God.*[30]

Closely related to robust metaphysical realism is Willard's second concern: *epistemic realism.*[31] The idea behind this concept is that it is possible to come in contact and interact with this invisible reality. J. P. Moreland connects epistemic realism to the notion of knowledge by acquaintance that we discovered earlier. This means we can know spiritual reality not just theoretically, but personally, interactively, and relationally.

Central to Willard's thought is the belief that experiences of truth itself are crucial to the life of the disciple. This kind of life "requires being able to be directly aware of God and his voice, an awareness that is prior to our interpretation of it."[32] To connect epistemic realism to Willard's bibliology, we might consider Scripture as a written, physical witness to robust metaphysical realism. We can connect with this reality—the idea behind epistemic realism—through immersion in Scripture realistically and experientially. To expound on this critical commitment, Willard wrote the books *Hearing God: Developing a Conversational Relationship with God* and *The Spirit of the Disciplines: Understanding How God Changes Lives.*[33]

Approaching the Bible in this realistic way should affect the entirety of the human person, because "human beings are uniquely designed (in particular because of their non-material aspects) to know God through direct experience."[34] This thought lies at the heart of Willard's third primary concern, *complete anthropology.*[35] Willard provides in-depth treatment of this subject in his landmark book *Renovation of the Heart: Putting on the Character of Christ.*

As these commitments become reality, a person's character undergoes identifiable and measurable change into Christ-likeness, leading to closer *communion* with God, which will result in greater *union* with him. This transformation lies at the heart of Willard's final primary concern.[36] As Moon notes, if each of Willard's "first three concerns is correct, then Christian spiritual formation and its practices should become established as a field of genuine knowledge."[37] This, in turn, could provide objective ways of testing the effectiveness of these formational practices. In sum, Willard's fourth primary concern is *the establishment of Christian spiritual formation as a domain of genuine knowledge.* He addresses this key theme in *Knowing Christ Today: Why We Can Trust Spiritual Knowledge.*

With this framework of Willard's four critical concerns in mind, we are now prepared to explore his idea of *biblical realism* more precisely. Moreover, we can identify the factors that have led to its demise—even among Bible-believing Christians. Willard develops the idea of biblical realism most fully through different sections of *The Spirit of the Disciplines.*

Willard introduces the concept as it relates to the role the Bible plays in the spiritual life. "Upon a realistic, critical, adult reading, by those prepared to be honest with their experience, the Bible incisively lays bare the depths and obscurities of the human heart." Why is this? Because Willard believes the Bible presents real portrayals of human lives that have experienced profound spiritual transformation. He adds, "This is why it [the Bible] continues to play the decisive role it does in human

history and culture and why it is fitted to be the perpetual instrument of the Spirit of God for human transformation, as
2 Timothy 3:16-17 indicates."[38] Reading the Bible as if what it
says can *realistically* happen today—to you, to me—is essential
for cultivating the Christian spiritual life.

In a later chapter titled "St. Paul's Psychology of Redemption,"
Willard probes more deeply into the necessity of biblical realism by exploring what he describes as Paul's *stern realism*.

> We today rest upon many centuries of interpreting his
> [Paul's] words and the words of other biblical writers in a
> fanciful, sentimental, or "spiritual" manner. His often
> quoted words, "I die daily," for example, have been turned
> into an expression of an attitude or spirit of self-sacrifice
> and humility.[39]

In contrast to this, Willard believes the context of Paul's expression of dying daily "makes it amply clear that for him this
wasn't an attitude but a daily fact of life—one in which he daily
stared death in the face and accepted it for that day, as we can
see in 1 Corinthians 15:30-32."[40] Realistic reading is not to be
mistaken for *literal* interpretation either. Willard makes this
point clear by noting Paul did not literally crucify his flesh to a
cross with nails, but he did take definitive action regularly to
deny his flesh.

Beyond this, Willard contends that many of the phrases Paul
uses over and over in his writings—including the ideas of spiritual life and death, putting off the old person and putting on
the new, union with Christ, and others—have become so familiar to contemporary Christians that they have lost their true
meaning, force, and substance.[41] Paul's intended meaning of

these phrases can be recovered by interpreting them through the lens of stern realism—realities that we can and should experience in ongoing renovation of our hearts.

Pivoting from Paul, Willard goes on to consider biblical realism from the perspective of John's Gospel. For instance, the great "union" passages (14:10-20; 15:1-10; and 17:20-26) "are explicitly about real interactions and personal conditions and their concrete results. But most of us find great difficulty in translating 'abiding in Christ and his words abiding in us' into familiar events of our daily lives. Yet this is precisely what *must* be done."[42] In other words, experiencing *communion* with God, which leads to greater *union* with him, should be the pursuit and expectation of the follower of Jesus.

Willard then boldly states that correcting *unrealistic* Bible reading is the urgent mandate for ministers of the gospel today. "Our most serious failure today is the inability to provide effective pastoral guidance as to how to live the life of Jesus. And I believe that is due to this very real loss of biblical realism for our lives."[43] Willard further clarifies the principle of reading the Bible realistically by describing the factors that have contributed to its demise among readers of Scripture.

Perhaps the most potent factor Willard identifies that has led to the modern loss of biblical realism is the dominant ideology of modern psychological thought, which has had the tendency to blunt or altogether undermine the realism of biblical language about the human self.[44]

In its efforts to be what is regarded as scientific, psychology tends not to accept religious experience and behavior as realities to be investigated on a par with other psychological phenomena. Many practitioners in psycho-analytic tradition deriving from Sigmund Freud still regard treatment as having failed if the client retains belief in God.[45]

Given this, Willard suggests that many Christian psychologists remain intimidated by this naturalistic bias and are therefore "unable to approach Christian behavior and experience as realities to be investigated in their best experimental and theoretical manner."[46] If some fields of psychology have little to no place for religious experience, and the culture we find ourselves immersed in is highly therapeutic, is it any wonder why so many Bible-believing Christians rarely read the Bible realistically? To combat this prevailing trend, Willard wrote the final book in his corpus, *Knowing Christ Today: Why We Can Trust Spiritual Knowledge.*

To be clear, Willard was not opposed to Christians availing themselves of psychotherapeutic support. His wife, Jane, in fact, worked as a licensed marriage and family therapist. Many Christian psychologists, including Gary W. Moon, consider Willard's *Spirit of the Disciplines* and *Renovation of the Heart* among the best works for understanding the human person. What Willard was against in much of modern psychological thought is its denial of the possibility and reality of religious experience.

Beyond the naturalism inherent in much of modern psychology, Willard also surprisingly attributes the loss of biblical realism to some of the greatest literature in the English language. Specifically, the cultural pervasiveness of the allegorical writings of John Milton and John Bunyan have unintentionally led many readers of Scripture to read biblical stories allegorically instead of realistically. While Willard is not criticizing the works of authors like these as *literature*, he is disturbed by the adverse effects they have had not only on how people have come to read the Bible, but in the passive way works like these have led followers of Christ to approach their spiritual growth. Willard maintains, "The impression is conveyed that this 'progress' will somehow automatically take place through the normal course of life, if only the pilgrim holds on to certain beliefs."[47] Here we see why transforming the way Christians read the Bible is indispensable to the advancement of the spiritual formation movement.

A final factor in the decline of biblical realism is due to what Willard views as "the church's gradual loss, over the centuries, of the reality of Paul's experience of Christ."[48] While Willard does not pinpoint precisely when in church history this "gradual loss" began to occur, the evidence is clearly and readily seen in the gross lack of transformative discipleship in the church today.

Additionally, to explore Willard's philosophical approach to interpreting Scripture, we must examine his primary philosophical specialization, phenomenology. According to Michael Stewart Robb, phenomenology is a method of gaining "comprehension of some reality by reflectively going into one's own experience."[49] Moreover, it's a way to understand subjective experiences in ways that are not subjective.[50]

Perhaps the best example of a biblical interpretation that results from Willard's phenomenological background is his definition of the kingdom of God. According to Willard, the kingdom of God is "the range of God's effective will, where what he wants done is done."[51] Through reflection on his personal experience, Willard discovers he has a kingdom—a personal domain that he has genuine say over. It is the range of his effective will. It is where what he wants done is done. To illustrate this, Willard would commonly ask people in his classes to hold up their purse or wallet. This—Willard would say—is the range of your effective will. You have genuine say over what goes in here. Based on these reflections on our individual kingdoms and his experience with and study of the four Gospels, Dallas reaches the understanding of the kingdom of God he writes about in *The Divine Conspiracy* and taught throughout his life. As we place our individual kingdoms within God's kingdom, we can enter into an eternal kind of life now.[52]

The practical implications for how Willard's philosophy impacts how Scripture could and should be read and experienced will become clearer as we explore how Willard read the Bible as a practical mystic.

READING AS A MYSTIC

By describing Dallas as a *mystic*, Moon writes in *Eternal Living*, "I simply mean that he believed God is present in a real sense and that when you talk with him a two-way conversation is possible."[53] Mystics, in other words, are those who, when they talk to God, believe in the possibility that God will talk back. Willard's approach to reading Scripture as a mystic began early in his life, first as a college student at Tennessee Temple.

During a holiday break from class, Dallas found himself virtually all alone on what felt like a deserted campus. While he didn't have the money to afford the trip back to see his family in Missouri, his solitude did afford him an unexpected opportunity. While doing laundry, he passed the time by beginning to read the Gospel of John. After making his way through the first few chapters, something prompted him to read all twenty-one of its chapters in their entirety. Never before had Dallas endeavored to read a Gospel straight through. But as he gave God's Word his sustained, unbroken attention over several hours, he experienced God's presence in a real, close, transcendent way—perhaps every bit as spiritually real as Jesus was physically close to Nicodemus or the Samaritan woman at the well. Experiences like these led Dallas to conclude the Gospels are for today, and not for some age to come—as his dispensational upbringing had taught him.[54]

Through reflection on these subjective, mystical experiences with God in Scripture (remember: this is how Willard thought philosophically as a phenomenologist), Dallas eventually formulated the following idea about Scripture, which he writes about in *Hearing God*. "Scripture is a communication that establishes communion and opens the way to union, all in a way that is perfectly understandable once we begin to have experience of it."[55] Fascinatingly this progression from *communication* to *communion* to *union* is the same pattern which Willard believes growth in the Christian spiritual life follows.

To illustrate this point, Willard employs the metaphor of marriage. In such a relationship, initial casual conversations mature into deeper communion—being together—in which there is a profound sharing of thoughts and feelings. Communion progresses into union when distinctions like *mine* and *yours* evolve into *ours*.[56] To Willard, union with God—or his presence with us—consists primarily in a conversational relationship with God "as his friend and colaborer in the affairs of the kingdom of the heavens."[57]

This progression of God's redemptive work—from communication to communion to union—is precisely how Willard understands Scripture. God communicates to us through his Word. As we pursue his presence and open our lives to hear him speak, we encounter a greater possibility for being with him through the words and verses of the text. As communication turns toward communion—again and again over time—these experiences cultivate greater union with God. By God's brilliant design, Scripture is given to us in a form that opens up the possibility of transforming us into people who can experience union with him in an ever-deepening way.

Throughout *Hearing God*, Willard describes people who have had mystical experiences of God's speaking voice and presence in profound, even extraordinary ways. One person he highlights is his older brother, J. I. Willard. Dallas describes how his brother sensed a hand on his shoulder in the middle of the night and a voice speak to him, saying, "Feed my sheep." This experience led J. I. to embrace a calling to become a minister of God, a vocation he pursued for over thirty years.

Dallas goes on to describe how the presence of God almost overwhelmed J. I.'s consciousness, transforming aspects of his personality. This even impacted how J. I. related to Scripture. Dallas writes, "He was suddenly living in the study of the Bible, memorizing much of it without trying to do so, even though his days were spent in hard physical labor."[58] Stories like these are recounted by Dallas to help everyone capture a vision of what the experience of eternal living might be like for us. As we pursue God—whether through Scripture or other spiritual practices—we should believe that experiences like these will come.[59]

While I continue to read Scripture like a "presbycostal," I now do so by integrating Willard's experiential approach to my discipline of studying the text. Like a Southern Baptist, I trust the authority and infallibility of the text, knowing that *God never leaves it alone.* Like a philosopher, I read *realistically*, believing that what happened to the people in Scripture could and should happen to me. Like a mystic, when I open the text, I believe *the author is in the room.* He loves me and desires to share an ever-deepening conversational friendship with me.

EXPERIENTIAL EXERCISES

1. Based on Willard's experiential framework, how might you begin to read Scripture more like Dallas did? What impact might this make on your spiritual life?

2. Begin memorizing Colossians 3:1-17, which Willard views as one of the great formational passages of Scripture. Reflect on it through the following questions:

   • In what ways does this passage highlight Willard's first critical commitment: robust metaphysical realism, which insists the invisible world is real. Hint: focus on the teachings in verses 1-2.

   • Based on this passage, how would one interact with this invisible world? (This is Willard's second critical commitment: epistemic realism.) Hint: pay attention to what this passage instructs us to do and not to do.

   • Willard's third concern is complete anthropology. He espouses in *Renovation of the Heart* that to change the whole person, the individual parts must be changed. There are six key aspects of the person: thoughts, feelings, heart/will/spirit, social context, body, soul.[60] How does Colossians 3 invite us to experience transformation in these parts of who we are?

- Willard's fourth critical commitment is for authentic transformation that results from genuine spiritual knowledge. Based on Colossians 3, how would you know you are growing spiritually?

3. Have you had deeper experiences with God in Scripture like Dallas first did as a college student? If so, what were those experiences with God like?

3

Getting the Bible Through Us

Know your Bible. Generally speaking, seminary
training does not make people adept in working with the
Bible. Your life and your Bible should start forming
a seamless whole. Wear out your Bible. Read it in large
stretches, and repeatedly. Read the New Testament
in one go. Set aside time so that you can read through
the New Testament five times in one week. Take notes,
because you will get stuff that will be life-giving.

DALLAS WILLARD, "BECOMING THE KIND
OF LEADERS WHO CAN DO THE JOB"

DALLAS WILLARD MODELED FOR ME that it was okay to
dog-ear a book. But it wasn't easy to finally give myself permission to do so.

Books are sacred to me, and they always have been. My
grandmother was a librarian. Watching how she meticulously
and painstakingly cared for the books at our public library and
the novels and nonfiction works in her personal collection in-
stilled in me a reverence for the written word that I've never lost.
Books are to be treasured, organized, respected. Books are not

to be taken lightly, scribbled in, or worse—lest my family's last name become a self-fulfilling prophecy—ripped.

When I became a Christian and started reading the Bible intentionally, I was encouraged to highlight, underline, and circle important words in my student Bible. For the longest time, I only did so in pencil, in case my grandma saw my copy of the Scriptures and reprimanded me. Books, like nature, should be left better than we found them, right?

In college, Mortimer Adler's classic text *How to Read a Book* pointed out the flaws in my thinking. He insisted on the importance of reading with a writing utensil in hand. Marking books and writing notes in the margins actually facilitated greater engagement with an author's argument, aiding the learning experience.[1] Adler's admonition incited in me a book-reading rebellious streak. I started marking my books in ink.

But until studying with Willard, I never dared to bend or fold a page of a printed text. In our class, next to the transparency machine, Willard had a stack of classic Christian books—most of which were assigned reading for our course. These included Nouwen's *The Way of the Heart*, Calvin's *The Golden Booklet of the True Christian Life*, Murray's *Humility*, and a copy of Willard's NASB Bible.[2] These texts were heavily marked and dog-eared to such a degree that the thickness of these books nearly doubled from their original printing.

Dallas even did this with the books *he* wrote! Looking at how Dallas marked up his own books reminded me of Tony Campolo's infamous line in his "It's Friday, but Sunday's Coming" sermon: "I was preaching so good I was taking notes on myself!"[3]

After one of our sessions, struck by Willard's apparent disrespect to the printed word, I asked him why he dared to do such a thing. He warmly replied, "Dog-earing books helps me locate selections from works that I'm searching for more efficiently." Not only so, but he added, "Reviewing portions of books I've marked or folded enables me to better understand, remember, and recite what I've read more effectively." He encouraged me to do the same with *his* books. I took his advice to heart. The impact: I haven't stopped quoting Dallas Willard since.

Like the counsel found in Adler's *How to Read a Book*, this chapter explores how Willard's experiential framework translates to practical ways anyone—not just the philosophically inclined—can better read the Bible. The result will be learning to read the Bible *transformationally*, and not just *informationally*. By learning to soak ourselves in the Scriptures like Dallas did, my hope is that we wouldn't simply get through the Bible, but that the heart of the Bible would get through us.

THE INTEGRATIVE MOTIF OF SCRIPTURE: THE WITH-GOD LIFE

Alongside his friend Richard Foster, Dallas Willard taught spiritual formation to groups around the world through the ministry of Renovaré. Beyond its conferences, events, and institute, one of the greatest fruits of Renovaré is its publication of *The Life with God Bible*, which was originally published as *The Renovaré Spiritual Formation Bible*. The dream of this massive project was to create a study Bible that would approach Scripture from the perspective of Christian spiritual formation.[4] But it almost didn't happen.

Many renowned theologians and biblical scholars convened to shape the arc, direction, and focus of this Bible, but they reached little agreement as to how this should happen.

Amid the tension and frustration of those gathered, Dallas sat quietly until he was asked to offer his perspective. Throughout the centuries, theologians have long debated what the overall theme of Scripture is. Luther suggested it was justification by faith. Calvin contended it was the glory of God. More recently, theologians have made the case for the kingdom of God. What did Dallas think? Into which historic category did he land?

Once given his opportunity to weigh in, Dallas graciously suggested the unity of the Bible—its integrative motif—is found in the development of a *with-God life* here on earth. As Willard traced this idea from Genesis to Revelation in what he referred to as the Immanuel Principle, theologian Thomas Oden began transferring Willard's words onto a whiteboard, declaring that this project should be the with-God Bible.[5] Like many of Willard's ideas, the *with-God life* as a unifying theme did not contradict the historic conversation around the integrative motif of Scripture, but it did not fit squarely into one theological category either. Perhaps this is another example of how Willard *uniquely* read the Bible as a whole *philosophically* and *experientially*.

In his foreword to *The Life with God Bible*, editor Richard Foster describes the rationale behind the creation of this important study Bible. "We need a study Bible that will lead us step-by-step into the glorious and terrifying 'with-God' life, which, like Ariadne's thread, weaves its way throughout Scripture."[6] Crucial to understanding this principle, according to the editors—including Dallas Willard—is the belief that "the unity of the Bible is discovered in the development of life 'with God' as a reality on earth, centered in the person of Jesus."[7]

Throughout the tapestry of Scripture, *The Life with God Bible* shows the availability of a life with God throughout every period of biblical history, including life in the kingdom of God today.

The Life with God Bible is perhaps the best resource which explicitly attempts to apply Willard's bibliology as comprehensively as possible. Throughout every primary section of this study Bible, the editors insert one of Willard's most vital statements about interpreting the Bible: "The aim of God in history is the creation of an all-inclusive community of loving persons with God himself at the very center of this community as its prime Sustainer and most glorious Inhabitant (Eph 2:19-22; 3:10)."[8]

This Bible also offers an important contribution to Willardian bibliology because it identifies the fifteen key movements of the with-God life as taught by Dallas Willard. Below is a brief overview of the with-God life found in *The Life with God Bible*, gently adapted for our purposes. I invite you to take a few minutes to slowly read through these movements, allowing yourself time and space to imagine how this integrative, relational theme unfolds through the story of Scripture.

1. The People of God in Individual Communion (Genesis 1–11)

2. The People of God Become a Family (Genesis 12–50)

3. The People of God in Exodus (Exodus–Deuteronomy)

4. The People of God in the Promised Land (Joshua–1 Samuel 12)

5. The People of God as a Nation (1 Samuel 13–2 Chronicles)

6. The People of God in Travail (Job, Psalms of Lament, Ecclesiastes, Lamentations)

7. The People of God in Prayer and Worship (Psalms)

8. The People of God in Daily Life (Proverbs–Song of Solomon)

9. The People of God in Rebellion (1 Kings 12–2 Kings 25:10; 2 Chronicles 10–36; Isaiah; Jeremiah 1–36; Hosea; Joel; Amos; Jonah; Micah; Nahum; Habakkuk; Zephaniah)

10. The People of God in Exile (2 Kings 25:11-30; 2 Chronicles 36:20-23; Jeremiah 37–52; Lamentations; Ezekiel; Daniel; Obadiah)

11. The People of God in Restoration (Ezra; Nehemiah; Esther; Daniel; Haggai; Zechariah; Malachi)

12. The People of God with Immanuel (Matthew–John)

13. The People of God in Mission (Acts)

14. The People of God in Community (Romans–Jude)

15. The People of God into Eternity (Revelation)[9]

This framework of reading and interpreting Scripture invites readers to ask what is arguably life's most important day-by-day, moment-by-moment question: *Am I living a with-God life or a without-God life?* Reading Scripture is not just something we should do out of love *for* God; reading the Bible is an invitation to be *with* God. Since God never leaves the Bible alone, we should seek to recognize and respond to the stirrings of God as we read his Word. Willard believes we should read the Bible in this prayerful, contemplative fashion as a fundamental spiritual discipline.

THE SPIRITUAL DISCIPLINE
OF READING SCRIPTURE

With the 1988 release of *The Spirit of the Disciplines*, Dallas Willard became more widely known in the Christian community. In this landmark work, he states, "The Spirit of the Disciplines is nothing but the love of Jesus, with its resolute will to be like him whom we love."[10] The goal of practicing spiritual disciplines, then, is not to get good at things like prayer or fasting or service; rather, the goal of the disciplines is to provide an environment for us to encounter the transformational presence of God, so we might be filled more and more, and through and through, with the love of the Trinity.

Willard defined a spiritual discipline as "an activity undertaken to bring us into more effective cooperation with Christ and his Kingdom."[11] They're activities "undertaken to make us capable of receiving more of his [God's] life and power without harm to ourselves or others."[12] In other words, spiritual disciplines are things we can do to help accomplish what we cannot attain by direct effort or mere willpower.

To illustrate, while I cannot run a marathon today by simply *trying* as hard as I can, I could *train* my body through a months-long plan of disciplined running, stretching, and strength training to complete a 26.2-mile race. *Trying* hard would enable me to slowly and painfully make it miles into the course (and likely in need of a ride to the hospital). But *training* would empower me to finish the race.

There are two main types of disciplines for training ourselves to experience an ever-deepening life with God: *disciplines of abstinence* and *disciplines of engagement*. Disciplines of abstinence include solitude, silence, fasting, frugality, chastity, secrecy, and sacrifice.[13] By intentionally choosing to abstain from activities we'd normally engage in—like eating and drinking or speaking and socializing—God can strengthen our capacity to *not do* what the enemy might tempt us to do. Stated differently, disciplines of abstinence help us overcome sins of commission, or doing what we should not do. By refraining from our normal day-to-day activities, we can create the setting and space to encounter the presence of God more fully, without distraction.

Disciplines of engagement, on the other hand, include practices like study, worship, celebration, service, prayer, fellowship, confession, and submission. While disciplines of abstinence help to "counteract sins of commission," Willard writes, "the disciplines of engagement counteract tendencies to sins of omission."[14] By doing things we wouldn't ordinarily do, we strengthen our capacity—by God's grace—to do what we would typically resist or avoid, like sharing our faith or having a difficult but necessary conversation. Disciplines of engagement empower us to say yes to God's invitations to follow him.

This overarching discussion around how spiritual disciplines work prepares us to better understand how to read Scripture to experience what we referred to earlier as knowledge by acquaintance, as opposed to mere propositional knowledge, or knowhow. When we read Scripture as a spiritual discipline, we discover opportunities to move from reading *informationally* to reading *transformationally*.

Continuing his discussion in *The Spirit of the Disciplines*, Willard notes that the spiritual discipline of the study of the Word of God is the primary discipline of engagement to which disciples of Jesus are called.[15] In this discipline, we strive to see "the Word of God at work in the lives of others, in the church, in history, and in nature. We do not only read and hear and inquire, but we *meditate* on what comes before us."[16] While study may sound like a scholarly pursuit, Willard believes this practice is for everyone, done best within the overall fellowship of other disciples of Jesus.

Wise biblical study must involve "giving much time on a regular basis to meditation on those parts of the Bible that are most meaningful for our spiritual life, together with constant reading of the Bible as a whole."[17] Throughout Willard's teaching ministry, he provides examples of Scripture passages most applicable to our spiritual lives, including but not limited to Psalm 23; the Sermon on the Mount (Mt 5–7); the Lord's Prayer; all four Gospels; Romans 8; 1 Corinthians 13; Colossians 3; and 2 Peter 1.

Beyond deep reading of these particular texts and the entire Bible as a whole, Willard repeatedly emphasizes the importance of memorizing Scripture. In *Life Without Lack*, Willard contends that memorizing Scripture "is even more important than a daily quiet time, for as we fill our minds with great passages and have them readily available for our meditation, 'quiet time' takes over the entirety of our lives."[18] Memorization is a crucial way we can, as Psalm 16:8 states, keep the Lord always before us.

In *The Spirit of the Disciplines*, Willard demonstrates the importance of memorization not only for people individually, but for congregations collectively.

As a pastor, teacher, and counselor I have repeatedly seen the transformation of inner and outer life that comes simply from memorization and meditation upon Scripture.

Personally, I would never undertake to pastor a church or guide a program of Christian education that did not involve a continuous program of memorization of the choicest passages of Scripture for people of all ages.[19]

When I first read these words, I felt immediate resistance. How could I get an entire congregation to memorize Scripture when I struggle to memorize Scripture personally? When I've shared Willard's discipline of Bible memorization with groups, the biggest pushback I hear is: "But I'm just not good at memorization. I guess this doesn't apply to me." If you're feeling similarly, I hope this clarification will help.

By Scripture *memorization*, I do not believe Dallas means Scripture *recitation*. The word *memorization*—for many of us—likely evokes memories of being forced to recite Bible verses against your will in Sunday school, or of anxiously standing before a high school classroom recalling Shakespearean sonnets for a grade. But to Dallas, Scripture memorization is about internalizing God's Word so that it lives and moves and has its being in you. It's not about committing God's Word to memory so that you can impress others by your ability to recall lengthy passages word for word.

For those who feel burdened by the challenge to memorize Scripture, Dallas would encourage us to *memorize Scripture as you can, not as you can't*. To get started, begin with a simple phrase from Jesus' words, such as "Follow me" (Mt 4:19). Repeat these words several times, then keep them before your mind periodically throughout your day. Notice how these memorized words nudge you to be with Jesus in the car, or at work, or as you decompress at the end of the day. Pay attention to what you experienced as you remained mindful of God's Word.

From memorizing phrases, you can gradually make your way to entire verses, and even to lengthier passages. You may also discover that *the more you memorize Scripture, the more Scripture you will be able to memorize.* You're not on your own to do this, after all. God is with you. He would love to help you hide his Word in your heart. Simply ask him. And remember: Scripture memorization is an *invitation*, not an *obligation*.

HOW TO READ THE BIBLE

While in *The Spirit of the Disciplines* Willard provides an overarching view of how engagement with Scripture can transform us through the work of the Spirit and experientially connect us with the presence of God, in *Hearing God*, he states more explicitly how to approach an individual passage of Scripture. First, Willard teaches that Scripture should be read with a *submissive attitude*.[20] We are to read it for the purpose of obeying it and laying down any aspect of our lives that is incongruent with it. In our day and age when personal experience appears to have been given the greatest authority for leading and directing our lives, Willard would urge us to yield to Scripture rather than our feelings. As he states in *Renovation of the Heart*, feelings are good servants but disastrous masters.[21] We can resist this pull of the culture to yield to our emotions by reading Scripture submissively.

To read with a submissive attitude is to read "with a readiness to surrender all you are—all your plans, opinions, possessions, positions." This does not negate rigorous study of the Word; rather, we should "study as intelligently as possible, with all available means, but never study merely to find the truth and especially not just to prove something. Subordinate your desire to find the truth to your desire to do it, to act it out!"[22]

Second, Willard warns against trying to read too much of the Bible at once.[23] We are not to simply get through the Bible. Our goal is to get the Bible through us. In *Hearing God*, Willard provides counterintuitive yet freeing Bible-reading counsel.

> You may have been told that it is good to read the Bible through every year and that you can ensure this will happen by reading so many verses per day from the Old and New Testaments. If you do this you may enjoy the reputation of one who reads the Bible through each year, and you may congratulate yourself on it. But will you become more like Christ and more filled with the life of God? It is better in one year to have ten good verses transferred *into the substance of our lives* than to have every word of the Bible flash before our eyes.[24]

Yet, as noted at the start of this chapter, Willard believed there was a right time to read extensive portions of the Bible. Sometimes the best way to meet God through Scripture is through reflection on a single word or verse. Other times, it's by reading an entire Gospel at a time, or even all twenty-seven books of the New Testament.[25] The bottom line for Willard is that we "soak" ourselves in Scripture with unceasing regularity.[26] Employing a range of Scripture-reading approaches can help us do this best.

Third, Willard instructs, "Come to your chosen passage as to a place where you will have a holy meeting with God."[27] Unlike some hermeneutical or inductive Bible study approaches that seek to dissect the text, Willard directs our aim toward preparing to encounter the author of the Scriptures. While Willard does not challenge any of the methods traditionally associated with the study of God's Word, he seems to imply that they fall short of reaching the ultimate goal of nurturing communion with God. To ensure we create the space to meet God, Willard counsels, "Do not hurry. Do not dabble in spiritual things. Give time for each stage to play itself out fully in your heart. Remember, this is not something you are doing by yourself. Watch and pray."[28]

Fourth, as described in how Willard read the Bible philosophically, we should "read the biblical accounts as if what is described is happening to us."[29] Failure to read the Bible in a realistic fashion can lead to two common errors among Bible readers. Our perspective can devolve to see the Bible as merely a book of doctrine, containing nothing but abstract truths about God. When this occurs, a person might study the Bible constantly "without encountering God himself or hearing his voice."[30] The second error that occurs when we fail to read the Bible realistically is that we stop reading the Bible altogether. Or as Willard vividly describes, we choke "it down like medicine because someone told us that it would be good for us—though we really do not find it to be so." To grow in reading Scripture, "we must prayerfully but boldly use our God-given imaginations as we read the stories of people who encountered God." Furthermore, "we must pray for the faith and for the experiences that would enable us to believe that such things could happen to us. Only then will we be able to recognize, accept and dwell in them when they come."[31]

Finally, Willard offers a five-step outline for meditating on a text that represents his adaptation of the ancient practice of *lectio divina* (sacred reading):

1. Information: Read the passage of Scripture.
2. Longing: What in this passage do you want to be true in your life?
3. Affirmation: Affirm this longing is actually true in Christ.
4. Invocation: Ask that God would make these realities experientially known to be true in your life.
5. Appropriation: Notice how God is working to make these realities true in your life.[32]

Let's apply this process to one of Willard's most beloved passages, Psalm 23:1. In *Life Without Lack*, we discover Willard translates this text as, "The Lord is my shepherd; I lack nothing."[33] This translation would be step one or the "information" of Willard's process.

Step two would be expressing our desire personally and prayerfully that God would be our shepherd and that he would bless us with lives that lack nothing.

Step three would invite us to read this verse realistically—that if God is my shepherd, then even if it seems like there are things missing in my life, I genuinely lack nothing because he is with me.

Step four provides us with an opportunity to turn that affirmation into a prayer. For instance, we might pray, "God, I know in my mind that you are my shepherd and that I lack nothing. Help me to know this reality to be true in the depths of my soul. May I lead a life that lacks nothing."

Step five—appropriation to make it so—challenges us to imagine and live like this truth is the actual reality of our lives. One of the ways I have learned to do this is during moments where I feel insecure or inadequate. I pause and pray this verse boldly and repeatedly: *The Lord is my shepherd; I lack nothing. The Lord is my shepherd; I lack nothing.* As I say this slowly and confidently, I have sensed God's peace dispel my insecurity and bless me with a sense of confidence in him.

To this five-step process, Willard wisely adds, "When there is an inner agreement between our minds and the truth expressed in the passages we read, we know that we have part of the mind of Christ in us as our own."[34] Points of awareness like this are confirmations that we are experiencing communion with God, which leads to increasing union with him. It is for this end that we read Scripture.

HOW NOT TO READ THE BIBLE

Not only does Willard outline key principles for how to read Scripture; he shares many warnings about how *not* to read the Bible. One of the first cautions Willard raises is toward what he calls playing "Bible roulette." In Bible roulette, readers "allow the Bible to fall open where it will and then stab their finger at random on the page to see which verse it lands on. Then they read the selected verse to see what they should do."[35]

Related to this is what Willard refers to as the "it's-all-in-the-Bible" view.[36] While the Bible provides direct instructions and principles about what to do in many situations in our lives, it will not tell you what to do with most of the details of your life. "Our reverence for and faith in the Bible must not be allowed to blind us to the need for personal divine instruction within the principles of the Bible yet beyond the details of what the text explicitly says."[37]

A final warning for how not to read the Bible is what Willard calls *Bible deism*, which "holds that God gave us the Bible and then went away, leaving us to make what we could of it, with no individualized communication either through the Bible or otherwise."[38] While the Bible is a primary means by which God speaks, Willard cautions us from drawing the conclusion that it is the only way God might speak to us today.

Overall, the best way to learn to read Scripture like Dallas Willard is not by merely understanding how he read it, but by applying his Bible-reading practices. Before reading ahead, I encourage you to take dedicated time and space to experiment reading Scripture like Dallas did through the experiential exercises provided below.

As Richard Foster neared his eighty-third birthday, I had the opportunity to ask him how he reads the Bible in this season of his life. In response, a wide smile spread across his face, coupled with Richard's signature chuckle. "God has kept me in a single text for more than four months now," he said. "Each day and throughout each day I've just stayed with a word or phrase or two from the great psalm of praise Psalm 100."[39] I guess praising God doesn't need to be rushed, does it?

After a lifetime preaching, teaching, and experiencing God through the pages of his Word, I think it's fair to say the Bible has gotten through Richard Foster. Word by word. Day by day. Decade after decade. Listening to Richard reminds me that we're never too old, nor is it ever too late, for God's Word to get through us.

EXPERIENTIAL EXERCISES

1. How does reading the Bible *informationally* differ from reading it *transformationally*? What has been your experience reading Scripture in each of these ways?

2. Trace the theme of the *with-God life* through the library of Scripture by reading the following Old and New Testament verses: Genesis 5:21-24; 6:9; Exodus 33:14; Joshua 1:5; Judges 6:16; 2 Chronicles 17:3-4; Psalm 23:4; Isaiah 7:14; Matthew 1:23; 28:19-20; 2 Corinthians 6:16; Revelation 21:3-4. Remember Willard's counsel to come to your chosen passage as a place where you will have a holy meeting with God.

3. Willard suggests that we dedicate "much time on a regular basis to meditation upon those parts of the Bible that are most meaningful to our spiritual life, together with constant reading of the Bible as a whole."[40] Throughout Willard's teaching ministry, he provides examples of Scripture passages most applicable to our spiritual lives, including but not limited to Psalm 23; the Sermon on the Mount (Mt 5–7); the Lord's Prayer; all four Gospels; Romans 8; 1 Corinthians 13; Colossians 3; and 2 Peter 1. Take time over the next week to read through each of these passages. What impact might regular meditation upon these texts have on your spiritual formation?

4. Select one of the biblical texts most applicable to our spiritual lives (from question three) and commit it to memory. Practice reciting this passage one verse at a time throughout the day. Based on your experience doing this,

how might Scripture memorization enable "quiet time" to pervade more of your ordinary daily life?

5. Apply Willard's five-step adaptation of *lectio divina* (sacred reading) to 2 Peter 1:3-11.

- Information: Read the passage of Scripture.
- Longing: What in this passage do you want to be true in your life?
- Affirmation: Affirm this longing is actually true in Christ.
- Invocation: Ask that God would make these realities experientially known to be true in your life.
- Appropriation: Notice how God is working to make these realities true in your life.

6. Consider setting a day aside to read through an entire Gospel, all four Gospels, or even the New Testament. Reflect on how this lengthier period of reading helped you connect with God differently than an ordinary daily quiet time.

7. Listen to Dallas's teaching, "Study and Meditation," delivered at Rolling Hills Covenant Church in 1981.[41] In this message, Dallas emphasizes the importance of concentration, repetition and understanding as it relates to the practices of meditating on and memorizing Scripture. He also issues this statement that rings all-too-true in our churches today.

One of my greatest griefs as an evangelical Christian is that in so many churches where they profess to believe the Bible, no one knows anything about it because they haven't studied it and they don't study it. They are consumers of talks.[42]

Reflect for a moment: In what ways might I be too much of a consumer of Bible "talks," sermons, or podcasts (even of Dallas Willard's!), instead of being a student who studies Scripture personally?

4

Reading Scripture like Saint Ignatius

Thus some of the most profound treatments of discipleship to Jesus,
such as . . . the Spiritual Exercises of Saint Ignatius, presuppose
a special class of Christians for whom they are not written. But
if you simply lay that assumption aside . . . you will see that they
offer, in substance, precisely what we have been discussing in this
chapter: a curriculum, a course of training, for life on the rock.

Dallas Willard, *The Divine Conspiracy*

Just as I have endeavored to read Scripture like Dallas
Willard, I believe Dallas Willard endeavored to read the Bible
like Saint Ignatius of Loyola. While Dallas didn't quote Ignatius as extensively as I have quoted Dallas (I'm quite confident hardly anyone has quoted any other individual person as
much as I've quoted Willard!), the influence of Ignatius appears,
from my perspective, to reverberate throughout Willard's
teaching and personal Bible-reading practices.

Perhaps most explicitly, Willard had this to say about
the Ignatian Exercises in his endorsement of Larry Warner's
book *Journey with Jesus: Discovering the Spiritual Exercises of*
Saint Ignatius:

The Spiritual Exercises of Ignatius is one of very few works produced by followers of Christ that reliably guides those who have seriously put their confidence in Christ onto a path where what we Christians endlessly talk about becomes the reality of daily existence. This is because Ignatius guides the disciple into experience of the things we talk about. The reality stands out in the details of what is experienced.[1]

In the doctor of ministry program I completed in spiritual direction through Fuller Theological Seminary and the Martin Institute and Dallas Willard Research Center at Westmont College, my instructors Gary W. Moon, Trevor Hudson, and Christopher Hall traced essential spiritual formation themes found in ancient Christian spirituality, Ignatian spirituality, and the insights of Dallas Willard. In many respects, their efforts were an attempt to explore in greater detail what Willard stated at the start of *The Divine Conspiracy*: "In these three books [*Hearing God*, *The Spirit of the Disciplines*, and *The Divine Conspiracy*] there is very little new, though much that is forgotten."[2] Perhaps an aspect of what Willard believed has been forgotten—especially in Protestant circles—are Ignatius's contributions not only to spiritual formation but to Scripture reading in particular.

Connections between Willard and Ignatius became apparent to me from Trevor Hudson's lectures and his book *Seeking God: Finding Another Kind of Life with St. Ignatius and Dallas Willard*. I hope these connections demonstrate, first, how Willard's thought is not unique; rather, it follows in the footsteps of many great men and women of Christ throughout the centuries. And second, I hope Willard's connections to Ignatius will bring greater clarity and practical application to brief statements Willard made about Scripture reading but did not elaborate on. For instance, what did Dallas mean when he said to read the Bible by using our *imagination*? I hope questions like these—that you may have wondered about—will now be answered more fully. Before looking at five specific ways Ignatius of Loyola read the Bible similarly to Dallas Willard, I'll offer a brief biography of Ignatius and explanation about what his Spiritual Exercises are and how they teach us to read Scripture. Additionally, I'll share a brief encouragement for any Protestants who may struggle with the idea of learning from a Catholic like Ignatius.

One of the richest gifts writers like Willard, Eugene Peterson, and Richard Foster have given me is the courage to read and learn from voices outside of my evangelical tradition. A great temptation many like me face is potentially missing the *treasures* found in different Christian traditions, because we focus only on the *troubles* associated with them. While there is much I do not resonate with in Catholic theology and practice—and even with Ignatius—I must not allow these troubles to prevent me from discovering and gleaning from the rich treasures found in voices outside my tradition. Even Ignatius himself relied on other Christian traditions outside his own.[3] The Ignatian Exercises are undoubtedly one of these rich treasures.

SAINT IGNATIUS OF LOYOLA (1491–1556)

Born in 1491 in the Spanish city of Loyola, Ignatius was the thirteenth child in a family of minor nobility.[4] As a young man, like many in his day, he fantasized about the glories, pleasures, and notoriety found in the life of a valiant knight. These dreams led Ignatius to chase after worldly pursuits that were concerning to those closest to him. In fact, his good old aunt, a nun, once warned him, "Ignatius, you will not learn nor become wise until someone breaks your leg."[5] She never could have guessed how prophetic these words would prove to be.

On May 20, 1521, during a battle in Pamplona, Ignatius attempted to defend a fortress the French were attacking. Ignatius recounted that, after prolonged bombardments, a cannonball struck him on one leg, crushing its bones. Because it went between his legs, the other was seriously wounded as well.[6] For the next nine long months, Ignatius lived cut off from the world in the upper level of the Loyola manor house. Without any books of romance to read (which were not unlike erotic romance novels of our day), Ignatius read the only books he could acquire: *The Life of Christ* and *The Flower of the Saints* (very different from sexually explicit novels today!).[7] These works gave Ignatius a newfound vision of life—to pursue being a saint like Saint Francis or Saint Dominic. Without this humbling, "shattering experience," as Trevor Hudson describes it, it is impossible to know if Ignatius would ever have become the humble pilgrim he ultimately became.[8]

In his autobiography, Ignatius details what he experienced as he imagined devoting his life to the service of God and others, as the saints he read about did.

> When he thought of worldly matters, he found much delight; but after growing weary and dismissing them, he found that he was dry and unhappy. But when he thought of . . . imitating the saints in all the austerities they practiced,

he not only found consolation in these thoughts, but even after they had left him he remained happy and joyful.[9]

These initial experiences of "consolation," as Ignatius described them, shaped the arc and trajectory of the rest of his spiritual life. Ignatius learned the art of discernment—carefully paying attention to the interior movements of his soul. This inner awareness enabled him to grow in intimacy with Jesus, as he recognized what events and feelings hindered his spiritual growth, and what experiences and pursuits enhanced his union with the God who loves us and wants to share life with us forever. These reflections evolved into the formation of his Spiritual Exercises.

WHAT ARE THE SPIRITUAL EXERCISES?

The Ignatian Exercises were designed to help Christ-followers encounter God and grow in their experiential knowledge of him. The Exercises are not a book to be read, but a guide to be followed. While crafted for Ignatius's early followers, who grew to become the Jesuit order, they were never intended for Jesuits alone. Through prayer exercises built on the foundation of the Gospels—following Jesus' birth, early ministry, passion, and resurrection—retreatants (those who are engaged in the Exercises) are given the opportunity to grow in union with God by experiencing interior freedom from sin and disordered loves. The hope is that those who complete the Exercises will be able to respond more faithfully and generously to God's calling on their lives.[10]

While the Exercises are often given today in an intensive thirty-day retreat format, Ignatius designed them to be flexible and adaptable. Nearly everyone I know who has completed the

Exercises—including myself—has done them in the context of their daily lives, with the guidance of a spiritual director, over a thirty- to forty-week period.

After following Jesus seriously for more than twenty-five years, I can attest that the Spiritual Exercises have proven to be the most impactful curriculum of Christlikeness I have ever experienced. The reasons for this are best seen by unpacking the five key connections that I believe illustrate how Willard read Scripture like Ignatius.

IGNATIUS–WILLARD CONNECTION 1: VISION OF GOD

While we may not always be conscious of it, how we think about God shapes our approach to reading Scripture. As preparation for the Spiritual Exercises, Ignatius describes his vision of God in what is called, the *Principle and Foundation.*

> God who loves us creates us and wants to share life with us forever. Our love response takes shape in our praise and honor and service of the God of our life.
>
> All the things in this world are also created because of God's love and they become a context of gifts, presented to us so that we can know God more easily and make a return of love more readily.[11]

Based on this description of God, Ignatian scholar David Fleming, SJ, contends, "The God Ignatius would have us know is Love loving."[12] Given this understanding of the nature of God and his desire to share his love with us through all that has been made in this world, the common mantra of Ignatian spirituality has been *finding God in all things.*

As Willard set forth in *The Divine Conspiracy*, God's essential nature is love. Because of this, God is the "most joyous being in the universe."[13] What links Willard's connection more deeply to Ignatius is how Dallas uses refreshed Ignatian language to call apprentices of Jesus to find God in all things. For instance, chapter three of *The Divine Conspiracy* is captivatingly titled, "What Jesus Knew: Our God-Bathed World." He begins this chapter with words that sound like a modern-day Saint Ignatius:

> Jesus' good news about the kingdom can be an effective guide for our lives only if we share his view of the world in which we live. To his eyes this is a God-bathed and God-permeated world. . . . It is a world in which God is continually at play and over which he constantly rejoices. Until our thoughts of God have found every visible thing and event glorious with his presence, the word of Jesus has not yet fully seized us.[14]

Within this description of our God-bathed world, I'm struck by Willard's employment of the word *play*. Though he doesn't explicitly make this connection, I believe Willard is borrowing the usage of this word from a famous line of "As Kingfishers Catch Fire" by Jesuit poet Gerard Manley Hopkins: "for Christ plays in ten thousand places / Lovely in limbs, and lovely in eyes not his / To the Father through the features of men's faces."[15] Given these connections, I believe Ignatius's vision of God— either directly or indirectly—shaped Willard's own view of God. How we view God directly influences how we read his Word.

When you think of God, what images or feelings come to mind? Dallas was fond of a thought from William Law's *A Serious Call to a Devout and Holy Life*, which invites us to *think magnificently of God.*[16] Take a moment to pause now. Contemplate the magnificence of God as described in Psalm 145:3 (MSG): "God is magnificent; he can never be praised enough. There are no boundaries to his greatness." Recognize this magnificent God is *for* you—God the Father. This magnificent God is *with* you—God the Son. This magnificent God is *in* you— God the Spirit.[17]

IGNATIUS–WILLARD CONNECTION 2: INTERPERSONAL ENGAGEMENT WITH SCRIPTURE

Trevor Hudson contends that a primary key to the Spiritual Exercises is "interpersonal engagement" with God.[18] As we demonstrated earlier, there are three types of knowledge: (1) propositional knowledge, (2) know-how, and (3) knowledge by acquaintance. For Ignatius, the Spiritual Exercises involve gaining experiential, knowledge by acquaintance of God. To employ language we previously heard from Willard, Ignatius desires to guide retreatants from merely having *communication* from God in Scripture, to experiencing *communion* with him, leading all the way to greater *union* with God.

Ignatius believed we could interpersonally engage with God in Scripture through what he called a "colloquy," or little conversation with God. According to Ignatian scholar Kevin O'Brien, SJ, in the colloquy, "we speak and listen as the Spirit moves us."[19] In other words, after reflecting on a passage of Scripture, we talk to God like a friend would talk to a friend, or like a child would communicate with his or her parent. Hudson notes, "As we engage in colloquy, we reveal ourselves to Jesus and he reveals himself to us."[20] Thus in the colloquy, mutual self-revelation enables interpersonal engagement with God to development. The reason for this is not because we are giving God any new *information* he doesn't already have about the state of our souls when we share openly and honestly with him. But in talking directly with him, we are giving God more *access* to our hearts.[21]

This access we give to God through self-revelation is why I believe the Ignatian colloquy is a central way we move from *communication* to *communion* in how we read Scripture. Perhaps this Ignatian conviction—about the possibility of directly relating to and interacting with God—grounded Willard's philosophical approach to reading Scripture.

What conversation might the Lord be patiently waiting for you to have with him now? What has been consuming your mind or weighing heavily on your heart? Perhaps this very moment is an opportunity to speak with our magnificent God—to give him access to your inner life. God loves to meet you right where you are, right as you are.

IGNATIUS–WILLARD CONNECTION 3: KEEPING COMPANY WITH JESUS IN THE GOSPELS

The core of the Ignatian Exercises is an immersion in the Gospels. We meet Jesus at every stage of his life and develop personal experiences with him through his teaching, conversations, miracles, suffering, death, and resurrection. Not only were the four Gospels central to Ignatius's curriculum for Christlikeness, but as we saw earlier, immersion in the Gospels profoundly shaped Dallas Willard's spiritual life. The Gospels were so essential to Willard that he gave Trevor Hudson some advice that sounded quite unusual, at least at first.

In *Seeking God*, Hudson recalls an evening he shared with Dallas, in which he asked a list of prepared questions. The most surprising exchange went like this:

Trevor: Could you provide me with a list of the formative books I should read?

Dallas: I suggest you read Matthew, Mark, Luke, and John.

Trevor: Okay, I have got that down. Are there any *other* books you recommend that I read?

Dallas: *(more emphatically)* My suggestion is that you take the next twenty years or so to read and mediate on these four Gospels. Read them repeatedly. Immerse yourself in the words and deeds of Jesus, and commit to memory as much as you are able.[22]

To practically read Scripture like Dallas Willard, follow this advice: *immerse yourself in the Gospels daily, repeatedly, deeply.* While I haven't been able to heed this advice for twenty years yet, I have spent time being with Jesus in the Gospels virtually every day for the past three years. Pondering the scenes, memorizing key texts, and sharing colloquies with Jesus throughout many sections of every Gospel have helped me—by God's grace—to cultivate an undeniably greater union with God. Keeping company with Jesus in the Gospels has enabled me, as Ignatius suggested we pray, to *know God more intimately, love him more intensely,* and *follow him more closely.*[23]

Keep company with Jesus in the Gospels for a moment now. Hear Jesus say these words to you: "Come with me . . . to a quiet place and get some rest."[24] Envision going with Jesus to a life-giving, restorative place. Picture what it would be like to see

Jesus unbusy, unhurried, totally content. How is this experience drawing you to know him more intimately, love him more intensely, and follow him more closely?

IGNATIUS-WILLARD CONNECTION 4: IMAGINATIVE PRAYER

To keep company with Jesus in the Gospels, Ignatius recommends we employ *imaginative prayer*. To pray imaginatively, we compose the place and setting of where an event with Jesus occurred, noticing as many details of the sights, sounds, tastes, smells, and feelings of the scene as we can. The hope: for us to enter these Gospel stories ourselves.

According to Kevin O'Brien, "Ignatius was convinced that God can speak to us as surely through our imagination as through our thought and memories."[25] This is because imaginative prayer allows the mind to descend to the heart—having the effect of stirring up thoughts and emotions that we can share with God in the form of a colloquy. This type of imaginative, prayerful reading is what Willard advocates for when he states in *Hearing God*: "We must prayerfully but boldly use our God-given imaginations as we read the stories of people who encountered God."[26] Reading Scripture imaginatively can have the effect of enabling us to encounter God more personally ourselves.

In *Seeking God*, Trevor Hudson tells a story about reading Scripture imaginatively that has transformed my approach to engaging the Bible, which I first heard him share with our doctoral cohort at Serra Retreat in Malibu, California, in 2019. While on an Ignatian retreat, Trevor was given the assignment by his spiritual director to spend time being with Jesus in

John 21. (This is the passage where Peter is reinstated by Jesus after his denials, and asked, "What is that to you?" after being overly concerned with the future of his rival disciple, John.) As he looked for a place to pray, he came across the retreat center's library. There he discovered fascinating commentaries of John's Gospel that captivated his attention.

As Trevor took extensive notes from these commentaries, he imagined how impressed his spiritual director would be when he revealed all he had learned from John 21. When it was time for the retreat director and Trevor to meet again, Trevor went through page after page of insights he gleaned from the commentaries, until the director finally interrupted him. He said to Trevor, "*Insight* is the consolation prize. *Encounter* is the grand prize."[27] In other words, Trevor pursued *informational* knowledge of this passage of Scripture, when his assignment was to interact personally and experientially with Jesus through imagination.

In our social media–saturated digital age, there seems to be no shortage of sermon *insights* attractively designed to be viewed and shared on Instagram and other platforms. Yet despite the staggering proliferation of wise, memorable, and sharable insights, they've had little to no positive impact toward increased growth in Christlikeness among Christians. Yes, we are more conversant and familiar with the impressive insights made from a wider range of thinkers and leaders. But I believe these insights are not leading to the kind of transformation we pray for the church to experience, because insight is only the consolation prize.

For preacher types like me, this means we must not settle for simply feeding our people memorable, pithy statements in our sermons. We must teach Scripture in a way that enables encounters with God to occur. For that to happen, we must not settle for reading Scripture to find great preaching insights. We must read Scripture for the ultimate purpose of encountering God first ourselves. Meeting God in Scripture through the use of imagination is a primary way we can do this.

One of the most poignant encounters I experienced while making my way through the Spiritual Exercises occurred as I sought to be with Jesus in Luke 2:41-52, where he is a twelve-year-old boy at the temple. Following Ignatius's instructions, I imagined what it would have been like to be with Jesus during this experience. To do so, I felt prompted by the Spirit to imagine that my twelve-year-old self was Jesus' friend. I imagined us having hung out together, gone to school together, shared meals and stories and jokes with each other.

At this point in our friendship, we seemed to be nothing but mutual friends—peers totally on the same playing field together. But then, I watched as Jesus got swarmed with attention at the temple. The most renowned scholars were staggered by his knowledge; the crowds were won over by his wisdom. He was going first-century viral for all the right reasons. (Insert mind-blown emoji here.)

Then I began to notice what my twelve-year-old self started to uncomfortably feel as this scene unfolded. It seems odd to say, but I suddenly felt strangely *jealous* of Jesus. That's right: jealously welled up in my emotions as I watched Jesus steal the limelight.

The emotions that rose to the surface of my soul through this form of imaginative reading naturally necessitated a colloquy— or a serious chat with Jesus about what happened. As I gave Jesus access to what I felt, he revealed truths about my heart that

I initially didn't want to hear. Why was I jealous of Jesus? Because I wanted to be the kind of person who gained attention for his walk with God, his insight into Scripture, his wisdom beyond his years. As I reflected on this further, perhaps I was jealous of Jesus because I wanted myself to be the hero of my story, not him.

Through continued reflection, it didn't take long for me to realize that I can be more jealous of the ministries of my peers than I want to admit. Coming to terms with this reality gave me the opportunity to repent of my inward sinful disposition and ask God to heal me of my pathological sinfulness. This colloquy also enabled me to find freedom in Willard's wonderful counsel: trust God and let go of the outcomes. (We'll explore this idea more in chapter eight, "Teaching Scripture like Dallas Willard.")

Sometimes encountering God's presence is comforting and consoling. Other times it's disruptive and disorienting. In seeking the grand prize of encounter, I am not seeking a specific kind of encounter with God; I am seeking God. I'll leave it up to the Creator to determine what kind of encounter his creature needs to experience.

Imaginative prayer opens the possibility for encountering God. And far more than insight, encounter leads to the transformation we need most. This is why we must never settle for reading Scripture *informationally*. We must insist on reading it *transformationally*.

Imagine for a moment that Jesus is asking you what he asked Peter in John 21: "What is that to you?" Have you been comparing your life to others in an unhealthy way? Where might there be jealousy in your heart like there is in mine? Now hear

Jesus say to you, like he did to Peter: "Follow me." What do you feel as you hear Jesus' commissioning words?

IGNATIUS-WILLARD CONNECTION 5: REFLECTION

A final way Willard approached Scripture like Ignatius was by reading and engaging it *reflectively*. According to David L. Fleming, SJ, Ignatian spirituality is "a reflective spirituality."[28] Woven inseparably into the fabric of the Spiritual Exercises is the prayer of examen. While Ignatius understood that his followers may sometimes miss longer set times of prayer, he was insistent that people never miss the examen.[29] The examen is an invitation to pause and review the events of the day (or given time period) in a spirit of prayerful reflection.

The examen that Ignatius outlined in the Spiritual Exercises comprises five key components:

1. Be grateful for God's blessings.

2. Ask the help of the Spirit.

3. Review the day, looking for times when God has been present and times when you have left him out.

4. Express sorrow for sin and ask for God's forgiving love.

5. Pray for the grace to be more totally available to God who loves you so totally.[30]

Prayer in this reflective way supports interpersonal engagement with Scripture, providing additional opportunities to recognize and respond to God's call through Scripture as it intersects with our daily lives.

While I'm not aware of any times Dallas specifically stated the prayer of examen was an essential part of his life with God, *reflection* undoubtedly was. As we learned about Willard's mystical experiences with God through Scripture as a college student, his reflections on these experiences led him to conclude that the Gospels were not for another era, but for today. Moreover, this bent toward reflective spirituality is also connected to Willard's philosophical focus of phenomenology. As a reminder (in case you're not able to easily rattle off a definition of this preposterously intimidating term), phenomenology is a method for seeking to gain comprehension of some reality by reflectively going into one's own experience. In other words, reflection on our subjective experiences is a source for obtaining objective knowledge.

For instance, we learned how Willard's reflections about what a kingdom is led him to define the kingdom of God as "the range of God's effective will." Given Willard's philosophical focus and his deeper, mystical experiences with God, we can see how the importance of reflection is another way Willard's posture toward Scripture and prayer is similar to Ignatius.

What has your experience with God been like lately? When has he felt close? When has he seemed absent? Reflect with God about what your life together with him has been like.

While Willard said many things that sounded new to his readers, they were deeply rooted in the lives and works of many saints of the past, including Ignatius of Loyola. One of the best next steps for learning to read the Bible like Dallas did may be for you to prayerfully consider working through the Spiritual Exercises of Saint Ignatius with a spiritual director. This experience was pivotal for my spiritual formation and for being able to more practically understand Willard's *communication* to *communion* to *union* pathway of meeting God in Scripture.

EXPERIENTIAL EXERCISES

1. Reflect: What Christian tradition—if any—do you come from? What did this tradition teach you about living as Christ's disciple? (Goal of this question: look for the treasure—not the trouble—in your tradition.)

2. How did Ignatius and Willard view God? What attracts you about these views? How do these views differ from the perspective of God you were taught or maintain?

3. From what we've learned in this chapter, how might you experiment with reading Scripture like Ignatius?

4. Read Mark 10:46-52 imaginatively. Imagine Jesus asking you this question: "What do you want me to do for you?" How would you respond? Share a conversation or *colloquy* with Jesus about it. Reflect on your conversation with Jesus. What stirred within you as you spoke and listened to him?

5

The IMMERSE Method

*It [the Bible] is the most profound book in human history by
far—by far—but that means you have to dig. You have to live
with it. You have to learn and grow and develop the concepts
and watch how it comes along. Then, it's really very rich.*

DALLAS WILLARD, *HEARING GOD*

AT AGE THIRTY-EIGHT, I relearned how to run. Now at this
point, I was far from a novice. I had been running three to four
times a week for over a dozen years. I had finished a full marathon and completed several other half marathons. But
somehow, I did all of that running—thousands upon thousands
of miles—unaware that I was not using proper form.

I gained recognition of this after an early Saturday morning
group run with members of my church. Close to fifty of us were
training to run the New Hampshire Half Marathon to raise
support for clean water with our global ministry partner, World
Vision. As we sat on the concrete parking lot, cooling down and
stretching after an eight-mile run, I shared with the team why
I had only run *one* marathon and not more: my feet tended to
go numb while running long distances.

To correct this issue, I had tried every remedy I could think of. Nothing worked. This forced me to accept that I had hit my running ceiling. I still loved doing it, but running any faster, any farther, any better was just not in the cards for me.

As I shared this struggle, my congregation members and teammates listened attentively and compassionately. I felt heard, even loved. Then, after a pause in the conversation, one of the newest members to the team, Troy, an elite athlete and running coach, spoke up. "Pastor Dave, you just have bad form."

After Troy subtly shared his perspective with the whole group, I asked him to show me—and the rest of us—how to do it right. Troy invited me to stand up. "Now," he said, "lean forward and let yourself fall until you naturally stop yourself by extending your leg forward." Not what I was expecting, but what did I have to lose? Here goes! I leaned forward, until my foot caught me from falling, and Troy said, "That, Dave, is the natural length of your stride. Rather than leaning back like you tend to do when you run, you should lean forward to the point that you almost feel like you're falling. That's lesson one."

"Thank you. What's lesson two?" I asked.

"You need to push off hard when you lift your feet off the ground—like you are propelling yourself forward," he said. "You tend to lift your feet off the ground like they are flat bricks. Instead, you need to rotate your ankles much more. That will allow the blood in your feet to flow more freely, and that's why your feet are going numb. You need to really *push off.*"

Several weeks after being taught this lesson—and focusing daily on my form—I ran twelve miles at a faster pace than normal without any numbing in my feet whatsoever. It was a breakthrough! I *relearned* how to run. Now, as excited as you might be for my running future, you might be wondering, "What does this have to do with reading Scripture like Dallas Willard?" I tell this story for these three reasons.

First, like my running for years, maybe you've felt like you've "hit the ceiling" when it comes to engaging Scripture. Sure, your daily devotions or inductive Bible studies have likely *worked* for you—and still could—but perhaps you haven't experienced any breakthroughs in your life with God for a while. Or possibly, you have felt yourself grow *numb* spiritually. You used to feel more spiritually alive—especially when you studied Scripture—but that passion has seemed to wane. If so, the "form" of Scripture reading that I'm going to explain might be the antidote you need.

Second, I'd like to challenge you to be willing to relearn how you read the Bible. Let me be the first to admit, relearning is one of the hardest and most humbling things you can do. It's hard because the longer you've done something, the more difficult it becomes to break the ingrained habits you've formed. It's humbling because the more experienced you are at something, the more challenging it can be to recognize and admit when and how you might be wrong.

Last, and most important, just as my running struggles resulted from a lack of "pushing off" to propel myself forward, my contention is that for us to read Scripture more like Dallas, we must "push off" from the words on the *page*, to go to the *person* of God himself. After all, the goal of reading Scripture isn't simply to know the Bible, but to know God more deeply and personally. In what follows, I will lay out an approach to reading Scripture that attempts to assimilate the key principles we have explored so far in a form that will enable us to "push off" from the *page* to the *person* of God. We will need God's help to do this, of course, and it will only happen by his grace. But I believe we have a role to play. It's our responsibility to position ourselves to meet with the author of the Bible when we open the pages of his book.

FINDING THE FLOW

While we will be looking at the steps that will enable us to go from the *page* to the *person*, it's important to keep in mind that for Willard, what we ultimately are after is the formation of a flow of relationship with God. He maintains that the spiritual life is not something you can cut up and make sense of, because the spiritual life is essentially a flow of relationship with the Father, Son, and Holy Spirit.[1] This is why Willard believed making disciples involves *submerging them in trinitarian reality*.[2] In other words, we are called to arrange our lives so that they are swept up in the flow of God's life. Willard believes this is possible—that God will guide us into the flow of his life—if we will only count on him for everything.[3]

What might this flow of relationship with God be like? To build on what we previously discovered, Willard describes the inner dynamic of the spiritual life as being a movement from *communication* that advances into *communion*, and from *communion* into *union*.[4] Like a river which flows toward the ocean, the communication–communion–union dynamic is a movement which flows toward an ever-deepening friendship with God. Fittingly, then, Willard defines Scripture by this very dynamic. "Scripture is a *communication* that establishes *communion* and opens the way to *union*, all in a way that is perfectly understandable once we begin to have experience with it."[5]

What exactly does Willard mean by these ideas of *communication*, *communion*, and *union*? The meaning behind communication for Willard is fairly straightforward. It is God speaking to us, primarily—though not exclusively—through Scripture. It's important to note that God continues to communicate with us even when we are living in opposition to him. He is always communicating; we just aren't always listening.

The purpose of God's communication is for it to flow toward greater *communion* with him. "When communication between two people rises to the level of communion," Willard writes, "there is a distinctness but also a profound sharing of the thoughts, feelings, and objectives that make up our lives."[6] Communion, or being together with God, like being with and sharing life with those we love, ultimately leads to *union*.

One of the strongest biblical metaphors for union is Jesus' teaching on the vine and the branches, found in John 15. In *Falling for God: Saying Yes to His Extravagant Proposal*, Gary W. Moon writes, "God wants us to be as close to him as a branch is to a vine. Connected. United. One an extension of the other. With a vine and branch, it is not possible to tell where one starts and the other ends. It is to be the same with God and us."[7] Like a branch that constantly draws sustenance from a vine, so our lives are to flow *from* God, *with* God.

Moon describes the moments where we have felt inseparably connected to God—whether in nature, at a worship service, or on retreat—as *unitive experiences*. "Unitive experiences have made drunks sober and caused hard-nosed academics—like C. S. Lewis—to be surprised and forever changed by the experience of pure joy."[8] The goal of learning to experientially read Scripture like Dallas Willard is to *push off* from the pages of the text (God's communication to us) by being with God as we read and meditate on his Word (communion) for the ultimate purpose of cultivating greater union with God himself. While complete union with God will not occur until Christ returns, an *eternal kind of life* with him is still available to us *now*.

INTRODUCING THE IMMERSE METHOD

How might we read Scripture in a fashion that naturally flows from communication to communion, all the way to union? We have already examined the glimpse Willard provides in *Hearing God*, his suggested approach or adaptation of the ancient form of sacred reading known as *lectio divina*. To review, the five steps of his approach are: (1) information, (2) longing for it to be so, (3) affirmation that it must be so, (4) invocation to God to make it so, and (5) appropriation by God's grace that it is so.[9] Beyond outlining these steps, Willard does not allocate much space to expand on this fivefold approach to reading Scripture. Perhaps this is his invitation for readers to determine how to follow this method on their own.

Through my own efforts to do this, I have formulated an approach to reading Scripture that combines Willard's five-step approach with the dynamic of communication–communion–union. The result is what I call the *IMMERSE method*. IMMERSE is an acronym that attempts to distill the different streams, creeks, and rivers that join as a confluence to create the flow of communication–communion–union. This acronym stands for Immersion, Meditation, Memorization, Encounter, Response, Supplication, and Experience. Think of each of these seven steps as tributaries that flow into the larger rivers of communication and communion, and these two rivers ultimately converging and flowing as a single river into the ocean of union with God.

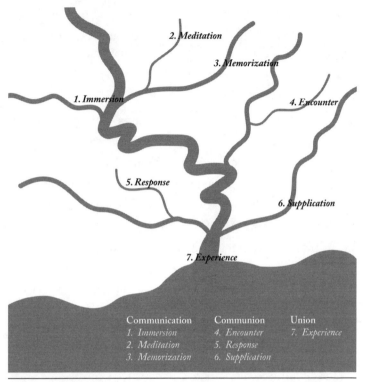

Communication	Communion	Union
1. Immersion	4. Encounter	7. Experience
2. Meditation	5. Response	
3. Memorization	6. Supplication	

The IMMERSE Method

Let me admit that a seven-step process feels like a lot. Undoubtedly, it is. But reading Scripture in this experiential fashion is not something that can be done casually or learned quickly. It will not only take deliberate intentionality, but also requires rigorous intensity and practice as well. This approach to reading Scripture is a lot like learning to master a musical instrument. At first, you're simply trying to learn how to play the notes, the major and minor scales. Unless you're a musical prodigy, it's hardly enjoyable at all. But once the scales and chords become ingrained, you can begin to play without having to think about what you're playing. You do it more easily and routinely. You're no longer concentrating on playing notes and scales and chords; you get swept up in playing songs, making music.

This progression from *scales* to *songs* to *music* is what we are attempting to cultivate as we explore what notes compose the scales of *communication*, and what scales and time signatures creates songs or *communion*, and what songs create a whole style of music or *union*. The point here is to encourage you to practice the IMMERSE method like you would a musical instrument before you write it off or give it up. Let me be clear: this is no small endeavor. IMMERSE is my attempt to synthesize nearly everything Dallas Willard said about reading Scripture into an approach that is logical, applicable, memorable, and even sharable.

While I am presenting IMMERSE in a step-by-step fashion, it is far from a *linear* sequence that must always be followed in this order. I am teaching these seven steps similar to how you would learn a major scale in music. If you're conversant with basic musical theory, this might sound familiar: *whole, whole, half, whole, whole, whole, half.* This progression describes the steps between the notes that make up a major scale. While it's essential to learn this in order to gain musical proficiency, these notes should *not* always be played in this order. Music that does not deviate from the progression of notes in a major scale would sound rote, predictable, boring.

When it comes to reading Scripture like Dallas Willard, the last thing we are aiming for is predictability or monotony. Perhaps the reason you're exploring this approach is because your reading of Scripture has grown uninteresting—if you're willing to be honest. The IMMERSE method is like learning a musical scale that will enable you to play seemingly endless melodies as you arrange and interchange and combine the individual notes. My hope in sharing this approach, then, is not for you to simply master the method, but for you to cultivate what Willard calls a "conversational relationship" with God through your engagement with the Bible.[10]

COMMUNICATION

Communication with God is established through immersion, meditation, and memorization. We will look at these three steps individually to discover how they form a confluence of conversation with God.

Immersion. Before we begin reading Scripture, we must approach the text with the proper posture of reverence and expectancy. When we read Scripture, we aren't just reading any other book or any other article we might view on our digital devices. We are reading the very words of God. Willard believes God's Word is *infallible* precisely because God never leaves it alone.[11] If God never leaves it alone, then when you place the words of the text before you—visually or audibly—the author of the book is in the room. God is with you. The profound nature of this mysterious reality should naturally lead us to nurture a sense of reverence, awe, and respect for God's interaction with his written Word.

In *The Allure of Gentleness*, Willard suggests we should reverently pray this prayer as we prepare our hearts to receive the Word of God: "Beyond the sacred page I seek Thee, Lord. My spirit pants for Thee, O living Word!"[12] Praying propels us from the page to the person.

What might this mean for you practically? For me—as much as possible—I try to prepare myself to read Scripture by finding a place that feels a bit set apart from the normal settings of my life. In our home, this place is the study I finished and furnished above our garage. To get there from our bedroom, you must first walk through our closet. (And yes, since I am unashamedly nerdy, I sometimes imagine this closet to be like C. S. Lewis's wardrobe which leads to Narnia.) The calm and quiet of this room—virtually soundproof because of our closet—feels almost like a monastery when compared to the flurry of sound and activity throughout the rest of our home. Sacred spaces are not just discovered; sacred spaces are made.

Once I enter this room, I often try to acknowledge the presence of God in some way. Following Dallas's example, I'll simply say to God, "You are here." And similar to Dallas's experience, occasionally I'll sense God whisper back, "Yes, I am." Other times, when I feel like I need to decompress from the chaos around our home, I'll practice what has been affectionately called *Willard walking*. Dallas often walked with his hands held together behind his back. It caused him to walk more slowly and reverently—also symbolizing that his defenses were down. Sometimes I'll walk around my room this way. It slows down my body and calms my soul in anticipation of meeting God in Scripture.

My experiments in nurturing reverence have taught me this: *you cannot hear a still small voice without first being still.* In *Hearing God*, Willard asserts that "the still small voice—or the interior or inner voice—is the preferred and most valuable form of individualized communication for God's purposes."[13] Given the primacy of hearing the still, small voice of God—the voice Elijah hears in 1 Kings 19—nurturing reverence is integral, not incidental, to reading Scripture like Dallas Willard. Reflect for a moment: before you rush into checking the "read the Bible" box off your to-do list, how might you carve out a few moments to be still and know that he is God (Ps 46:10)?

After first preparing to immerse in Scripture by nurturing reverence, we ready our hearts, or *expect* that we might encounter God in a real and experiential way. To enhance our sense of spiritual expectancy, Willard offers this suggestion: "Come to your chosen passage as to a place where you will have a holy meeting with God."[14] In other words, Scripture is not simply a book to be studied. Scripture is a gateway to God and his kingdom.

As we approach the text, Willard encourages readers to *reaffirm our participation in biblical experience.* "It is worth reminding ourselves to read the biblical accounts as if what is described is happening to *us.* We must make the conscious effort to think that such things *might* happen to us and to imagine what it would be like if they were to happen."[15] This statement is a prime example of Willard's *realistic* approach to reading Scripture. To read the Bible realistically, we must read it *expectantly.*

Willard continues, "We must be open to the possibility of God's addressing us in whatever way he chooses, or else we may walk right past a burning bush instead of saying, as Moses did, 'I must turn aside and look at this great sight and see why the bush is not burned up'" (Ex 3:3).[16] One of the most common tendencies for people who are well-versed in Scripture is to merely go through the motions when we read. When we study a familiar passage, rather than engaging it closely and deeply, we allow our attention to glaze over it, thinking we have already got it. While this is certainly unavoidable at times, when going through the motions of reading becomes our habit, we fail to be mindful that God's Word is, as Hebrews 4:12 emphatically states, *living* and *active*.

Like the preparations we make before a significant appointment or a first date, *reverence* and *expectancy* are postures we assume in order to ready ourselves to be in the company of God. Ultimately, reverence and expectancy help us have the humility needed for conversing with God. Willard writes, "Humble openness before the recorded Word of God is sufficient for receiving his saving and guiding word to us."[17] We may not need to devote extensive amounts of time for preparation, because sometimes even just a few moments of stilling our hearts and heightening our expectancy will make us ready to have a holy meeting with God.

Now that we have made the proper preparations for engaging in conversation with God through Scripture, we must decide what passage or passages of Scripture to actually read. In *Hearing God*, Willard provides us with wise counsel for making this choice: "Do not try to read a great deal at once."[18] He goes on to quote Madame Guyon: "If you read quickly, it will benefit you little. You will be like a bee that merely skims the surface of a flower. Instead, in this new way of reading with prayer, you must become as the bee who penetrates into the depth of the flower. You plunge deeply within to remove its deepest nectar."[19]

To begin reading Scripture by following the IMMERSE method, Willard would recommend we start "*with those parts of Scripture with which we have some familiarity*, such as Psalm 23, the Lord's Prayer, the Sermon on the Mount, 1 Corinthians 13 or Romans 8."[20] Or based on the advice Willard gave to Trevor Hudson, start with the Gospels. There is likely no better way to begin immersing ourselves in Scripture than by immersing ourselves in the words and actions of Jesus.

When selecting how much of the Gospels to read, most Bible translations identify individual units of Scripture by supplying a heading, written in bold font before the selected unit of Scripture. A single unit of Scripture is a good amount to read when beginning to learn this method. To get started, simply and slowly move through a portion of a chapter each time you read. You may find God inviting you to stay with a selected portion of the text for multiple days in a row. Listen to the Spirit's leading. Remember, the goal is not to get *through* Scripture, but to get Scripture *through us.*

Now that we have determined how to select a passage to read, let's explore how to *immerse* ourselves in the words of Scripture. In *Hearing God*, Willard urges us to read with a submissive attitude. To read submissively means having "a readiness to surrender all you are—all your plans, opinions, possession, positions."[21] In other words, don't read to merely find inspiration for doing what *you* want to do. Read Scripture in order to put into practice what it teaches. Read the Bible to *live* it.

In order to grasp how the Scriptures are calling us to live, we must do our best to interpret what they say. Willard believes it is necessary to "study as intelligently as possible, with all available means, but never study merely to find the truth and especially not just to prove something. Subordinate your desire to *find* the truth to your desire to *do* it, to act it out!"[22] How might we practically do this?

To begin, we should slowly read through our chosen portion of Scripture with as much concentration as we can. When we read things that appear to challenge how we are thinking or acting, we should pay special attention. This might be a way God is calling us to *submit* to his Word. Inevitably, as we read, there will be many things we find that we don't understand. For this reason, Willard encourages us to study *with all available means*. These would include things like study Bibles, commentaries, Bible dictionaries, and teachings from respected scholars and pastors. By *immersing* ourselves in a chosen passage, we are endeavoring to hear and understand what God is communicating through the *text* and *context* of Scripture.

Meditation. After immersing ourselves in a given portion of Scripture, we *meditate* on it. To distinguish between these two ideas, I am using the word *immerse* to signify the kind of reading we largely do with our minds. By *meditate*, I am referring to the kind of reading that occurs as our minds descend to our hearts. In immersion, our goal is to get a sense of what the text means. In meditation, we are listening for what the text means for us *personally*.

In *The Spirit of the Disciplines*, Willard says,

> We not only read and hear and inquire, but we *meditate* on what comes before us; that is, we withdraw into silence where we prayerfully and steadily focus upon it. In this way, its meaning for us can emerge and form us as God works in the depths of our heart, mind, and soul.[23]

This, obviously, is not a part of the process that can be rushed. In fact, Willard says, "We devote long periods of time to this. Our prayer as we study meditatively is always that God would meet with us and speak specifically to us, for ultimately the Word of God is God speaking."[24] Because there are a lot of competing cultural views of what meditation is in our day and age, let's home in on what Willard means by meditation.

At one of the meals I shared with Dallas during his 2010 Denver Seminary course, I specifically asked him, "Can you explain what you mean by *Christian meditation*?" What I recall from Dallas's response is this: In New Age and eastern forms of meditation, the focus is on *emptying* our minds of all thoughts. "In Christian meditation," Dallas said, "the focus is on *filling* our minds with thoughts of God and his Word." The reason for this is significant. In *Life Without Lack*, Willard claims, "The most important thing about us is our mind. . . . And the most important thing about our mind is what it is fixed upon."[25] This means what we give our attention to shapes who we become. In meditation, then, we are fixing our fullest and best attention on God and his Word.

To go from immersion to meditation, we listen for what words or phrases in the passage the Spirit draws to our attention. We listen for the inner, still, small voice of God and wait patiently for him to speak. We respond by humbly and submissively devoting our concentration to what God brings to mind. The practice of meditating helps us move from *communication* to *communion* in the *flow* of our relationship with God through Scripture.

Memorization. Alongside meditation in the IMMERSE method is the practice of memorizing Scripture. According to Dallas, Scripture memorization was the single most important spiritual discipline in his life. In fact, he said, "I would not be a pastor of a church that did not have a program of Bible memorization in it, because Bible memorization is a fundamental way of filling our minds with what they need."[26]

How did Scripture memorization affect Willard's life so profoundly that he insisted on it in the local church? According to Steve L. Porter, "As Dallas memorized the text, he interpreted and applied it, allowing the Spirit of God to breathe the life-giving, nourishing meaning of the Word of God into his heart/spirit/will."[27] As a result of this transformative process, Willard asserted, "Memorizing Scripture is even more important than a daily quiet time, for as we fill our minds with great passages and have them readily available for our meditation, 'quiet time' takes over the entirety of our lives."[28]

Not only did memorization help Dallas experience ongoing "quiet time," but this discipline aided his understanding and interpretation of Scripture. New Testament scholar Michael J. Wilkins believed Willard had the most intuitive grasp of the actual meaning of Scripture of anyone he ever met.[29] This intuitive grasp of Scripture was the direct result of how the Spirit worked through Dallas's discipline of memorizing Scripture. Memorization enabled the internalization of Scripture to occur in a profound way. As he lived with Scripture internally, it allowed him to acquire a sense of its deeper meaning.

In many ways, Willard's approach to teaching Scripture—from the overflow of his memorization of God's Word—is reflective of how the Law was read to the people of Israel in Nehemiah 8:8: "So they read from the book, from the law of God, with interpretation. They gave the sense, so that the people understood the reading." One of the ways Willard uniquely communicated Scripture through his lectures and books is through the manner in which he gave its sense. That sense was not only heard in his words but felt through his personal presence. He lived and experienced what he taught.

If I had to boil reading Scripture like Dallas Willard down to one point of application, it would simply be: *memorize as much of Scripture as you possibly can, as consistently as you can.* Make memorization the cornerstone habit of your engagement with the Bible. Start with the most formational passages we noted (Psalm 23; the Sermon on the Mount; the Lord's Prayer; Romans 8; 1 Corinthians 13; Colossians 3). Then focus your attention on the Gospels. The progression from *immersion* to *meditation* to *memorization* enables our reading of Scripture to flow from communication to communion.

COMMUNION

"When communication between two people rises to the level of communion," Willard writes, "there is a distinctness but also a profound sharing of the thoughts, feelings, and objectives that make up our lives."[30] Every step in our approach so far has involved a sense of communion or being with God. Now at this movement in our approach, we are concentrating on *pushing off* from the pages of Scripture, to go to the person of God himself. To go from communication to communion in our IMMERSE method, we will explore the next three steps in this flow of relationship: *encounter, response, supplication.*

Encounter. As Trevor Hudson said, *insight* into Scripture is the consolation prize to our reading, while *encountering* God's presence is the grand prize. To encounter God interpersonally through Scripture, we must employ our God-given faculty of imagination. Through imagination, we no longer stand at a distance from the text; we find ourselves as participants in it.

For instance, as we participate imaginatively in Scripture, we no longer hear Jesus asking *others* questions like, "What do you want?" (Jn 1:38 NIV); we hear Jesus asking us personally, "What do *you* want?" As we spend time with God by engaging Scripture like it's happening to us, we can commune with God more fully and freely.

One of the most memorable encounters with God I've had occurred through the reading of Psalm 121. Before beginning my role as lead pastor of Crossway Christian Church in March 2019, I went away for a retreat at Camp Brookwoods in Alton Bay, New Hampshire, along the southeastern shore of Lake Winnipesaukee. This place is sacred to me. I've been privileged to baptize dozens of people in Winnipesaukee's beautiful waters. I've shared transformational conversations with people I've led on retreat. At Brookwoods, *unlike* Jacob in Genesis 28, I've known God *is* here and have relished being in his beautiful presence.

As I prepared my heart for the unknown journey of spiritual leadership before me, I spent time on retreat immersing myself in, meditating on, and memorizing Psalm 121. I imagined God being my "keeper," finding help in him amid the future ministry challenges that would inevitably come. Most striking, though, was how Psalm 121:8 came alive to me: "The LORD will keep your going out and your coming in from this time on and forevermore."

I imagined God keeping my "going out" through my efforts to transition from my previous ministry role at Grace Chapel in Lexington, Massachusetts, as faithfully as I possibly could. I reflected on the conversations I had, the goodbyes I shared, the blessings we as a family received. God kept us.

I then imagined my "coming in"—the future sermons I'd preach, the staff meetings I'd lead, the challenges I knew were waiting for me. God blessed me with a sense of his presence through it all. While he didn't completely shield me from ministry attack or absorbing blows from others, he never left my side for a moment. I felt not only kept but swept up in the flowing current of God's unceasing love.

During all the grueling, gut-wrenching challenges of leading through the pandemic, I looked back on this encounter with God in Psalm 121 almost every single day. I proclaimed the truth and undeniable reality: God *is* my keeper. I am being kept now. In the moments I doubted the likelihood that I would make it very long in this role (during the most intensive and divisive moments of 2020), God assured me that he would be my keeper through any and every "going out" or "coming in."

To be candid, encountering God in a very tangible way like this is more of the exception and not the norm for my regular reading of Scripture. Most often, my times of Bible reading feel ordinary, not extraordinary. It would be accurate to describe my everyday experience to be far more reading Scripture like Dave Ripper than reading Scripture like Dallas Willard.

But I have still found this principle to prove true: *God shows up to the degree that I let him.* If I give God two to three days of my unhurried time and uninterrupted attention, I sense his presence far more profoundly. If I give God twenty minutes of my time before a busy day, he will certainly meet with me, but my experience of his presence will be far less intense.

For these reasons, Dallas encouraged apprentices of Jesus to experiment spending great lengths of time reading through an entire Gospel, or even the entire New Testament. By and large, the more intensely we seek God through Scripture, the more significant our encounters with him will be.

Response. Crucial to communing with God is *responding* faithfully and obediently to his leading. To begin to do this, it's paramount we pay attention to and notice what we are feeling and thinking as we pursue communion. To follow the lead of Ignatius, in this step, we want to pay particular attention to the inner movements of spiritual *consolation* and *desolation* that we experience as we seek to be with God.

According to Ignatius, *consolation* describes God's movement to inflame our hearts with greater love for him or increase within us faith, hope, and charity. *Desolation* is essentially consolation's opposite. David Fleming, SJ, describes spiritual desolation as inner experiences of disturbance, darkness of soul, or feeling moved toward low and earthly things.[31] We might imagine feelings of spiritual consolation as things that draw us toward God, and spiritual desolation as feelings that draw us away from God. Noticing and talking to God about these inner movements, or feelings, can help us catch the current that will sweep us up into the flow of relationship with God. For God does not just meet us in our thoughts, but also in our emotions.

As a result of our immersing, meditating, memorizing, encountering, and noticing, God often calls us to act—to obey.

As Dallas comments on the Great Commission in Matthew 28, it is not enough to *know* what Jesus said; we must *do* everything he commanded. To emphasize the importance of this point, Willard postulates, "We have Bibles with red letters to indicate what he [Jesus] said. . . . Might we not make a good use of a Bible that has green letters for what he *did*? Green for 'go,' or 'do it'?"[32] Perhaps it would be advantageous to start reading the Bible through *green-colored* lenses.

At this point in our approach to reading Scripture, we may very well need to put down our Bibles and do something. This might first mean drawing closer to God himself. Central to

Willard's philosophy was the idea that *you can go to the thing itself*.[33] The second of Willard's four key concerns, *epistemic realism*, captures Willard's ardent belief that we can come into direct contact and interact with realities of the invisible world, such as the Trinity and the kingdom of God.[34] We can do so in such a way that we gain genuine knowledge from these interactions. This idea led Willard to contend that when Christians pray, Jesus will walk right up and engage them in conversation.[35] Perhaps our faithful response to our interpersonal engagement with Scripture is to be still so we can gain more knowledge by acquaintance, by experiential connection to God.

Another way to respond might be to boldly and obediently do what God is calling us to do. Engage in the difficult conversation you've been avoiding. Give generously toward the cause you've felt burdened to contribute to. Repent of an ongoing sin of commission or omission. Gary Moon refers to one of the most important Dallas-isms as "Dallas 3:16." In response to the question, "How does one become a saint?" Dallas would answer, "By doing the next right thing."[36] We respond in communion with God by doing the next right thing God is leading us to do.[37]

Faithful response to Scripture is essential to reading Scripture like Dallas Willard, because he was convinced, "The organ of spiritual knowledge is obedience. Just as you open your eyes to see colors, you know the presence of the kingdom of God by obedience."[38] In other words, only as you *go*, do you really *know*. Through obedient action, we encounter the reality of God's kingdom more fully.

Supplication. In Willard's adaptation of *lectio divina*, he underscores the importance of *invocation*, or asking for God to supply what we have heard in conversation through Scripture to be true for us. To do so, we may pray, "Lord, make it so for me."[39] For instance, if we are reading John 15:11, and we are meditating on Jesus' intention for his joy to be in us, and for our joy to be complete, in this step of the IMMERSE method, we directly ask Jesus to supply us with his joy. Prayers of supplication can be a way God is inviting us to faithfully respond to his Word.

Willard emphasizes this important step by stating, "We must pray for the faith and for the experiences that would enable us to believe that *such things could happen to us*. Only then will we be able to recognize, accept, and dwell in them when they come."[40] This is an example of what Dallas means by instructing us to read Scripture *realistically*. It's also a call to pray Scripture *boldly*. In this example, we must believe that Jesus really wants us to experience his joy and pray that he would supply what we need for his joy to be complete in us.

Continuing to use John 15:11 as an example, let's hypothesize for a moment that the joy of Jesus—or whatever another text might be inviting us to experience—is not something we really *want* to ask Jesus for. If so, then we can ask God to give us the desire we do not have. We can talk to God about why we don't desire what he's inviting us to receive.

Now some of us might be feeling resistance toward the idea of asking God for something that's for *me*—especially so directly. Willard claims in *The Divine Conspiracy*, though, that prayer is essentially a *request*.[41] Willard writes, "What prayer as asking presupposes is simply a personal—that is, an experientially interactive—relationship between us and God, just as with a request of a child to parent or friend to friend."[42] What often happens as the result of one person making a request to another? In many cases, it's the deepening of the relationship.

When a member of my congregation asks to talk and we agree to meet, we almost always leave feeling more connected to one another than we did before. Had this person not asked, we would not be experiencing the closer connection that we now have. The same is true for our relationship with God. Asking God to supply what we need paves the way for us to experience closer communion with him.

To make this personal, what have you been reluctant to ask God for? Perhaps your resistance to asking has unintentionally created a barrier that is keeping you from experiencing greater intimacy with God. If so, allow God to break through these walls of relationship with him, by simply asking him to do so. As we strengthen—and flex—our asking muscles, we will be able to push off from communication with God through Scripture to deeper communion with God himself, leading all the way to greater union with him.

UNION

Deeper experiences of communion with God ultimately lead to greater *union* with him. As we move from communication with God through Scripture to communion with him, we gain *experiential* knowledge of God and his Word. Let's examine the final step of the IMMERSE method, *experience*.

Experience. The flow of Scripture reading that begins with immersion ultimately results in *experiential* knowledge of God. We don't just know more *about* God; we know him personally, intimately, and interactively. To use John 17:3 as a familiar example, we don't just know about the possibility of eternal life;

we experience *eternal living* here and now. Another way Dallas Willard describes experiential knowledge is as *self-authenticating* knowledge.[43] It's knowledge that we know to be true because we have experienced its reality undeniably. For instance, we can know that the Lord really is our shepherd in a self-authenticating way because we've experienced his presence with us while we were walking through the valley of the shadow of death. We know that he shepherds us because he has led us to green pastures or still waters. When broken, burned out, or depleted, we have experienced God restoring our souls. Our experience of engaging Scripture authenticates its reality in our lives.

During the most intense moments of the Covid-19 pandemic, like many pastors, I was met with a lot of suspicion by different congregation members. Having been the lead pastor of our church for only fifty-two weeks before the pandemic began, I'd had very little time to build the trust needed to lead our church through these divisive, uncertain days. Along the way, disinformation about my character began to spread. During this time, rather than seeking to retaliate or expend a lot of energy attempting to defend myself, I decided to put into practice Dallas Willard's thought of *trusting God with your public relations department*.[44]

To be completely honest, there were certainly moments when I didn't think God knew much—if anything—about public relations. But I channeled my fears, worries, and insecurities into praying Psalm 26:1: "Vindicate me, O Lord, for I have walked in my integrity." By simply conversing with God about my need for vindication and asking him for it, over time I began noticing small ways God *was* vindicating me. Through wisdom given by mentors, God was guiding me through the wilderness. From the support of staff, elders, and key leaders of the church, God protected me through these storms. Now, reflecting back on the past years of ministry, it is evident God forged a stronger, healthier church through the crucible of our shared sufferings. This vindication of my character and ministry has given me *self-authenticating* or *experiential* knowledge that God can be trusted. And vital to any deepening, uniting relationship is trust.

This self-authenticating knowledge was not something I became aware of immediately. It developed as I reflected on the trials I endured. Reflection is essential to gaining the kind of experiential knowledge that deepens our trust in God. As a phenomenologist, Willard believed we could gain comprehension of some reality by going into one's own experience of it.[45] In this final step of the IMMERSE method, then, we are invited to look back over our experience with God as we pursued him through the steps of this process: (1) immersion, (2) meditation, (3) memorization, (4) encounter, (5) response, (6) supplication, (7) experience. Our reflections on this process of reading and *living* a particular passage provide us with personal, self-authenticating knowledge. This type of knowing enables us to enjoy shared experiences with God through his Word. To put this all together—because relationships are built on shared experience, this approach to reading Scripture is designed for us to share experiences with God, which leads to greater union with him.

But like any healthy relationship, transformative shared or "unitive" experiences are given, not forced. We don't gain deeper experiences with God by seeking God for the sake of the experiences. We are called to seek God for God himself.

In *Seeking God*, Trevor Hudson shares a letter he received from Willard in 1995 regarding this important point:

> I encourage you to seek the face of the Lord constantly, with the knowledge that experiences will come along. You should experience God. I would be nothing and have no faith apart from various experiences of God that have come to me. You should expect experiences and make yourself available to them. To seek them is just misguided, not wrong. We have no idea of what ours will be like, and they certainly will be unlike anyone else's.[46]

Experiential knowledge of God is—like grace—a sheer gift. We can do nothing to earn it or achieve it. But grace, as Willard frequently stated, is "opposed to earning, but not to effort."[47] The IMMERSE method is not a process that can earn experiential knowledge or greater union with God. But it is a pathway that, through rigorous effort and intensity, wedded with grace, can lead us to encountering God's presence in an ever-deepening, transformative way.

APPLYING THE IMMERSE METHOD

When teaching IMMERSE, I've often been asked, "How long should this approach take to complete?" While the answer varies from person to person, generally speaking, I think it's best to allocate no less than thirty to forty-five minutes to follow the flow of the seven steps. While that's a good time frame to aim for, I've had experiences where I felt swept up from *communication* to *communion* to *union* in as little as ten to fifteen minutes. But that's been the exception, not the norm.

On some occasions, I've experienced the power of the IMMERSE method over the course of a day, not just in one sitting. For instance, in the morning, I might dwell exclusively in the communication steps of immersion, meditation, and memorization. Then, amid the course of my day, some event might invite me to commune with God—allowing me to encounter his presence through the theme of the text. That encounter will call forth a response and often necessitate a prayer of supplication—asking for God's help to do the next right thing. As I review my day at night, my reflections often lead to more acutely felt experiences of God's presence as I notice how God has woven together his Word and my work, and times of solitude with community and service.

If you're anything like me, if an activity or task is not scheduled, it's often not done. I'd recommend scheduling times to practice the IMMERSE method like you would schedule runs on a marathon training plan. Typical training plans include shorter runs each week, a couple mid-length runs, and one long run. The common marathon training advice I've been given is: *don't miss your long runs*. It's okay to miss your shorter runs on occasion, but make every effort to ensure you don't miss your long run. The long run is how you gain the endurance and distance needed to complete the course.

Similarly, I encourage you to read Scripture consistently and daily. But at least once a week, I recommend you set aside a much bigger block of time—an hour or two, or even more—to curate sacred space and time to apply IMMERSE. Some days won't afford the opportunity for unhurried time to be guided through these seven steps. But at least weekly—or as much as you are able—be sure not to miss your long run.

Also like group running, you might experiment doing IMMERSE in community. While Dallas spent a considerable amount of time studying Scripture alone, he also did Bible studies with others. You might consider practicing the experiential exercise below with a friend or small group. You might also consider meeting with a spiritual director to reflect on your experiences with God in Scripture. We need spiritual friends to help us recognize and respond to God's sacred stirring through his Word.

EXPERIENTIAL EXERCISE OF THE IMMERSE METHOD

Like relearning to run, we can only grasp the IMMERSE method by doing it. As practice, I'd invite you to follow this seven-step process with Matthew 11:28-30 as your chosen text.

In preparation, nurture a sense of reverence for the text you are about to read and heighten your sense of expectancy for how you might meet God in Scripture. Then *immerse* yourself in this passage by reading it several times. Consider the secret of the easy yoke by reading Willard's commentary on this passage in chapter one of *The Spirit of the Disciplines*. To whet your appetite for further study, Willard says the secret is "the intelligent, informed, unyielding resolve to live as Jesus lived in all aspects of his life, not just in the moment of specific choice or action."[48] What aspects of this passage is God inviting you to *meditate* on? Are there phrases of this text—or all of it—that you can work toward committing to *memory*?

As you move from *communication* to *communion*, push off from the words of the text by seeking to *encounter* God. Imagine being called to come by a leader as humble and gentle as Jesus.

Notice what you're feeling as you receive his invitation to come to him. Consider how God is inviting you to *respond* obediently to his wild and wonderful invitation. How might you pray this text? What do you need God to *supply* to you so you can join in the work he is doing in and through you?

Finally, reflect on your *experience* of being with Jesus in this passage. How is he inviting you to become as close to him as a branch is to a vine? In what ways did you experience Jesus' rest?

Like developing proficiency on a musical instrument, the IMMERSE method will take dedicated time and practice to become more intuitive and less mechanical. But as you gain fluency with this approach, I believe you will find the flow of life with God through reading Scripture—from communication to communion, and from communion all the way to union.

6

Experiencing the Old Testament

The "gospel" of the Old Testament . . . was simply
"Our God reigns!"

D ALLAS W ILLARD, T HE D IVINE C ONSPIRACY

"W HY DOES THE G OD OF THE O LD T ESTAMENT seem so different from the God we find in the New Testament?"

When teaching people to read Scripture like Dallas Willard, this is one of the most common questions I am asked. Chances are, as you've read through the Bible, you have probably wondered this as well. I have. Even after years of theological training, it's a still a question I wrestle with.

In this chapter, I will attempt to address this question the way I believe Dallas Willard would. Coupled with this, I'll present Dallas's most enriching commentaries on portions of the Old Testament. While it's beyond the scope of this work to present Willard's theology of the Old Testament comprehensively, I hope to give you a better sense of how he experienced the presence of God through these thirty-nine books. May you experience God through these beloved Old Testament passages like Dallas did.

MAKING SENSE OF THE OLD TESTAMENT IMAGE OF GOD

In *The Divine Conspiracy*, Willard shares one of his guiding principles for thinking theologically about Scripture. "The acid test for any theology is this: Is the God presented one that can be loved, heart, soul, mind, and strength? If the thoughtful, honest answer is 'Not really,' then we need to look elsewhere or deeper."[1] The reason for this is because God is a loving, competent, radiant being.

If the text in question does not present God as lovable, then where else should we look? Dallas would agree that we should interpret one part of Scripture with the whole of Scripture in mind. Given this, Willard would have us look to Jesus, of course.

In John 14:9 (NIV), Jesus is speaking to his disciple Philip when he says, "Anyone who has seen me has seen the Father. How can you say, 'Show us the Father'?" If we want to know what God is like, we need look no further than to Jesus. As Colossians 1:15 tells us, "He [Jesus] is the image of the invisible God." I like how Archbishop Michael Ramsey describes our God: "God is Christlike and in Him is no un-Christlikeness at all."[2] While I wholeheartedly believe this is true, it raises the question: Why does the God of the Old Testament appear at times to be so un-Christlike?

In *The Kingdom Among Us*, Michael Stewart Robb offers a perspective on how Willard might address this. He believes that Willard "thinks of the Bible as an inspired product of the progression through which God's people passed as they gradually came to understand God and his kingdom."[3] Thus, Willard discovers unity in the Bible "not because of its homogeneous theology—one constant understanding of Christ and other topics—but because the Bible is part of a long historical process that took place in the people of God, both Israel and the church." He concludes that the unifying principle of the Bible "is God's relationship with people over time."[4] Or to reframe this idea with Dallas's thoughts in *The Life with God Bible*, all of the Scriptures are about the *with-God life*.

The most unique way this idea is captured is through a small sentence Robb discovered in the notes to a lecture Willard gave in 1975. It states, "*in the Bible not progressive revelation but a revelation of progressive ~~application~~ apprehension*."[5] This note not only names the hermeneutical viewpoint Willard desires to distance himself from, but it reveals a window into his own process of wrestling with this issue.

While we find no explicit, in-depth elaboration of the concept of *progressive apprehension* in Willard's written work (to the best of my knowledge), Robb offers a helpful attempt to summarize what Willard might have had in mind. Robb contends that *progressive revelation* is distasteful to Willard because "if God is directly responsible for suboptimal views of himself, he is responsible for the application of those views in suboptimal living, to put it mildly."[6] Alternatively, Robb believes Willard perceives the Bible as presenting a *first listener's–eye view* of God and people's relation to him, rather than a *God's-eye view* of his relation to humanity. Therefore, Willard conceives of the Bible as being divinely inspired revelation, but a revelation "rooted in a people's *progressive apprehension* of their God and his kingdom."[7] While I am grateful for Robb's assessment of what Willard intended, which strikes me as reasonable and accurate, I lament the lack of Willard's own written explanation and development of this provocative concept.

Thankfully, though, Robb discovered an instance of Dallas speaking about progressive apprehension in a 1987 teaching Willard delivered during a retreat for Valley Vista Christian Community. In this discussion, Dallas applies his framework of progressive apprehension to the Old Testament accounts of (1) Achan and corporate guilt (Josh 7) and (2) the Israelites' harsh, seemingly inhumane treatment of the women and children affected by intermarriage in Ezra 9–10. In response to these passages, which appear to paint an un-Christlike portrait of God, Willard states, "All through the Scriptures we see a progressive apprehension of God."[8] I interpret this statement to mean that Dallas does not believe the leaders' responses to the people's sins, detailed in Joshua 7 and Ezra 9–10, reflect the heart and character of God. Rather, they reflect the leaders' incomplete apprehension *at that time* of who they believed God was, and how God would want them to respond.[9]

When readers of the Old Testament come across difficult passages like Joshua 7 or Ezra 9–10, I believe Dallas would encourage us to look "elsewhere" and "deeper" by reading "the Bible in conversation with itself." In *The Life with God Bible*, the editors—including Dallas—write, "The unfolding drama of Scripture often raises puzzling questions, which are resolved only when more obscure and difficult passages are held under the light of clearer, more straightforward passages." They add, "In this way the whole Bible guides us into a better understanding of its particular parts." If the unity of the Bible is captured by "the Immanuel Principle," as the editors believe, then we must read difficult Old Testament passages through the lens of Jesus, our God who is with us—the image of the invisible God.[10]

GENESIS 3: DEPRAVITY VERSUS DEPRIVATION

How does Dallas Willard understand what is commonly known as "the fall" in Genesis 3—where Adam and Eve eat the forbidden fruit? How does this impact us as human beings? In *The Spirit of the Disciplines*, Dallas addresses this issue. He observes that "there is some pervasive and basic lack in human life."[11] Then he raises the question, "*What* is human life being cut off from to leave it in such a sad and depleted condition?"[12] The answer: the spiritual realm. Willard elaborates by saying:

Disruption of that higher life [the spiritual] wrecks our thinking and valuation, thereby corrupting our entire history and being, down to the most physical levels. It is this pervasive distortion and disruption of human existence from the top down that the Bible refers to as sin (not sins)—the general posture of fallen humankind. Humans are not only wrong, they are also *wrung*, twisted out of proper shape and proportion.[13]

This wrongness and wrungness is the cause and effect of why human life is so deformed. This finds its origins in Genesis 3. Drawing on Robb's research, Willard describes the fall as "the leap." It is a "morally reprehensible intention of the human will to depend on something other than God. This chosen disposition cuts Adam and Eve off from 'the spiritual' which was meant to be a central external source of their existence, that on which they most depended."[14] As a result, human beings do not just suffer from moral *depravity* because of their sin, they also suffer from spiritual *deprivation*. Or to use Willard's words, "The evil that we do in our present condition is a reflection of a weakness caused by spiritual starvation."[15]

What is the remedy to this pervasive problem of sin? We not only need to be forgiven, but we need to experience what Dallas calls "the additional birth" Jesus speaks of in John 3.[16] We need to be reborn in order to be reconnected to the spiritual realm. According to Robb,

> The depraved human personality must be made alive to the spiritual world of God through faith so as to gradually bring the whole person into balance and order, with love of God, self, and neighbor as natural results.[17]

Regeneration is the beginning of this process, but it is sustained in a redemptive, healing fashion as our starved souls feed on and are nourished by life with God in his kingdom among us.

I appreciate that Dallas does not see our human problem only as moral depravity, but also as spiritual deprivation. We are cut off from the spiritual, and as branches, we must be reconnected and continually connected to the vine in order to overcome our pathological sinfulness, bear fruit, and flourish (Jn 15). In my life, this has transformed how I confess my sin and seek forgiveness. A common prayer of mine has now become, "Lord, forgive me of my sin (depravity) and heal me of my sinfulness (deprivation)."

NUMBERS 6:24-26: BECOMING A PERSON OF BLESSING

From February 21–23, 2013, my wife, Erin, and I, with hundreds of others, were privileged to experience Dallas Willard's final conference in Santa Barbara, California, before he died a few months later in May. His final talk was a call to the church to become people of blessing. It was the most radiant message I've ever heard.

To introduce Aaron's blessing in Numbers 6, Dallas, in keeping with his philosophical roots, gave us one more definition.[18] "Blessing," he said, "is the projection of good into the life of another." The act of blessing involves God, "because when you will the good of another person, you realize only God is capable of bringing that." Naturally, and perhaps intuitively, then, we say, "God bless you."

The church, Willard believes, should be a place of blessing. One of the challenges the local church must overcome to become this kind of community is our struggle to *receive* blessing. Willard said, "One of the problems in blessing is to get the other person to hold still enough to receive it." To overcome our inability to receive blessing, we must remember that blessing is an act of grace, not an act of indebtedness.

Having established this foundation, Willard then led us through Aaron's blessing line by line. Dallas prefaced his commentary by noting that if you try to improve on it, you won't make much headway. It is that rich, that beautiful—full of the love we see in Christ.

"The Lord bless you." This means, may "God bring good constantly into your life."

"The Lord bless you and keep you." Here we are stating, "God protect you. God build around you his safekeeping. The blood of Jesus and the Spirit of Christ be over you and keep you."

At this point, Dallas invited the group in attendance to begin practicing blessing someone near them—to experience this text. My wife and I turned toward one another. Dallas said to take turns looking intently into each other's eyes as you say, "The

Lord bless you and keep you." He insisted we emphasize *you* to the other person. The intimacy of this act was more intense than nearly anything I had experienced before. It was deeply moving, and after we exchanged those words of blessing, we let out a sigh of relief that this exercise was completed. But Dallas wasn't done.

"The Lord make his face to shine upon you." "One of the most precious things that we can have," Willard said, "is living before the shining face of God." If you struggle to grasp what a shining face is like, Dallas recommended finding a grandparent looking at their grandchild; then you will witness a face shine.

"The Lord be gracious to you." According to Dallas, *"Gracious* means the flow of love and his [God's] activity in creating what is good." Before moving on, he urged us again to slowly extend these words of blessing to each other—and *receive* these words of blessing as the gift they are.

"The Lord lift up his countenance upon you." Dallas interpreted this interesting phrase to mean, "May the Lord look right at you personally." Perhaps this is an opportunity for you to imagine God looking at you right where you are, right as you are. I'm confident his expression is radiating with love.

Finally, *"The Lord lift up his countenance upon you and give you peace."* "Peace," Dallas said, "comes in the presence of God, in having God's shining face over you and in having him looking to you." As our faces shone by giving and receiving blessing from one another, one of the most sacred senses of peace I've ever felt seemed to gently fall over every person in the room.

Dallas summarized this experience by stating that when we bless someone, "We're asking for an entire atmosphere of God's reality to be present on the person we are blessing under the invocation of God." What we felt that day in Santa Barbara was an atmosphere of God's present reality. No one wanted to leave. No one wanted Dallas to part—to leave this world. But thanks be to God that this man not only lived a radiant life, but blessed us with such radiant words, even as he neared a radiant death.

JOSHUA 1:8: WORTH MORE THAN A COLLEGE EDUCATION

Given Willard's repeated emphasis on the spiritual importance of Scripture memorization, should it be any wonder that Dallas loved Joshua 1:8 (NIV)? It states, "Keep this Book of the Law always on your lips; meditate on it day and night, so that you may be careful to do everything written in it. Then you will be prosperous and successful." Dallas's words about this text are among my favorite of all of his commentary on Scripture. In *The Great Omission*, he says,

> "The book of the law shall not depart out of your mouth" (Joshua 1:8). That's where we need it! In our mouth. Now, how did it get in your mouth? Memorization. I often point out to people how much trouble they would have stayed out of if they had been muttering Scripture. . . . You meditate on it day and night. What does that mean? Keep it, and therefore God, before your mind all the time. Can anyone really imagine that they have anything better to keep before their mind? No! . . . I often tell people I can give them one verse that is worth more than any college education, and it is Joshua 1:8.[19]

Coming from someone who was a college philosophy professor for forty-seven years, that is quite a statement! But

Dallas's dedication toward internalizing God's Word—and the profound impact it had on his thought and life—is one of the biggest reasons why you're holding a book about how he read Scripture.

PSALM 23: A LIFE WITHOUT LACK

No discussion on Dallas Willard's experience with the Old Testament would be complete without a special focus on Psalm 23. Along with the Lord's Prayer, Dallas prayed through this beloved passage line by line nearly every day. Because God really is our shepherd, Dallas believed a life that lacked nothing was genuinely possible.

In the posthumously released *Life Without Lack: Living in the Fullness of Psalm 23*, we are blessed to read Dallas's extensive thoughts on the kind of life our Great Shepherd makes available to us. Rather than overly comment on Willard's teaching, I'd like to close this chapter by inviting you to immerse yourself in this text, letting Dallas guide and direct you into God's presence, so you may enjoy communion with the Lord.

The Lord is my shepherd:
I'm in the care of someone else. I'm not the one in charge.

I shall not want:
That's the natural result. I shall not lack anything.

He makes me to lie down in green pastures:
What kind of sheep lies down in green pastures? One that has eaten its fill.

He leads me beside the still waters:

A sheep that is being led beside still water is a sheep that is not thirsty.

He restores my soul:
The broken depths of my soul are healed and reintegrated in a life in union with God: the eternal kind of life.

He leads me in the paths of righteousness for his name's sake:
The effect of the restoration of my soul is that I walk in paths of righteousness on his behalf as a natural expression of my renewed inner nature.

Even though I walk through the valley of the shadow of death, I will fear no evil:
A life without lack is one that carries no fear of evil, because of our confidence in God. It soars above wants and fears.

For you are with me:
The possibility of a life without lack is based on the presence of God.

Your rod and Your staff, they comfort me:
These represent the Shepherd's strength and protective care. I am at liberty to enjoy the overwhelming generosity of my Shepherd.

You prepare a table before me in the presence of my enemies:
Since I love my enemies, I would not feast upon a delicious meal in their presence and let them stand there hungry. The abundance of God's provision and safety in my life is so great, I would invite them to enjoy what God has prepared for me.

You anoint my head with oil:

He is not only interested in giving me something wonderful to eat, but also in blessing me with a life that is full and free and powerful in him.

My cup overflows:

I have more than my cup will hold. So much that I can be as generous as my Shepherd without fear of ever running out.

Surely goodness and mercy shall follow me all the days of my life, and I will dwell in the house of the Lord forever:

This is a description of . . . the abundant with-God life that comes from following the Shepherd, where we dwell and abide with God in the fullness of his life.[20]

EXPERIENTIAL EXERCISES

1. Take time to memorize Joshua 1:8. How might you keep God's Word before your mind more regularly?
2. Genesis 5:24 (NIV) says, "Enoch walked faithfully with God; then he was no more, because God took him away." Consider Willard's commentary on this passage below. How are Willard's words an example of what he means by reading Scripture *realistically*?

> Today I continue to believe that people are meant to live in an ongoing conversation with God, speaking and being spoken to. Rightly understood I believe that this can be abundantly verified in experience. God's visits to Adam and Eve in the Garden, Enoch's walks with God and the face-to-face conversations between Moses and Jehovah are all

commonly regarded as highly exceptional moments in the religious history of humankind. Aside from their obviously unique historical role, however, they are not meant to be exceptional at all. Rather they are examples of the normal human life God intended for us: God's indwelling his people through personal presence and fellowship.[21]

3. Read the Ten Commandments, as found in Exodus 20. Ponder Willard's commentary on this central teaching of Scripture:

> The Ten Commandments given to Moses are so deep and powerful on these matters that if humanity followed them, daily life would be transformed beyond recognition, and large segments of the public media would collapse for lack of material. Consider a daily newspaper or television newscast and eliminate from it every report that presupposes a breaking of one of the Ten Commandments. Very little will be left.[22]

4. Take unhurried time to pray Psalm 23 verse by verse, while incorporating Willard's teachings from this text into your meditation.

5. Following Dallas's example of being a person of blessing, how might you adopt his posture of blessing people interpersonally, or when given the opportunity to do so, more publicly in a worship service?

7

Experiencing the New Testament

When we open ourselves to the writings of the New Testament
. . . the overwhelming impression that comes upon us is that
we are looking into another world and another life.

DALLAS WILLARD, *RENOVATION OF THE HEART*

WHAT IS JESUS LIKE?

In *The Divine Conspiracy*, Dallas Willard dispelled the common misnomer that Jesus is merely nice. Rather, Dallas insisted, Jesus is *brilliant.*[1] He has the most trusted information on what matters most to the human condition. To read the New Testament like Dallas Willard, we must read it from the perspective that Jesus was the smartest person who ever lived. The Gospels and the letters of the New Testament offer the greatest answers to life's greatest questions.

In this chapter, we'll explore three ways that we can read the New Testament like Dallas Willard. First, we'll examine how the Gospels of Jesus should be read through the lens of the four great questions of life. Second, we'll examine Willard's extended translations of New Testament passages. Finally, we'll study Dallas's definitions for several key New Testament words.

To experience the New Testament like Dallas did, we are invited to think magnificently of Jesus.

THE FOUR GREAT QUESTIONS

As a master teacher, Jesus provides answers to the ultimate worldview questions pondered throughout human history. The first question Willard refers to as "The Reality Question."[2] This question asks, "What is real? What is reality?" The answer we find Jesus giving to this question is: *God and his kingdom.*[3] From firsthand experience, Jesus claimed to genuinely know this reality. As he states in John 16:28, he comes from the Father and is one with Father. His life, ministry, and teachings are invitations for people to align their lives with ultimate reality.

The second great question considers, "Who 'Has It Made'?"[4] According to Willard, this question investigates who is well-off or blessed. Jesus answers this question by contending that the blessed person is "anyone who is alive in the kingdom of God, that is, anyone who is interactively engaged with God and with the various dimensions of his reigning."[5] Jesus' description of the blessed life appears early in his ministry through teachings known as the Beatitudes, found at the start of his Sermon on the Mount.

The third great question Willard refers to as "The Character Question."[6] It considers who in our world is a good person. To this Willard claims, "A really good person, as Jesus teaches, is *anyone pervaded with love*: love for the God who 'first loved us' and who in his Son taught us what love is (1 John 4:9-11)."[7]

The final great question addresses how we might become people pervaded with Christlike love. Willard calls it "The Development Question,"[8] which asks, "How do you become a really good person?" According to Dallas, "You *place your confidence in Jesus Christ* and *become his student or apprentice in kingdom living.*"[9]

When we read the Gospels and hear Jesus' invitation to follow him, we should know he is calling his prospective disciples to enter into *reality*—what's really real. He's inviting them to experience the *blessed life* by becoming a person *pervaded with agape love.* The path to becoming this kind of person, who experiences this kind of life, is by *becoming Jesus' students*, his *apprentices* or *disciples*.

The New Testament is not just a volume filled with nice stories about a nice savior. It contains the best answers to life's greatest questions, taught by the most brilliant person to ever live. Obedience to these teachings brings the abundance of life Jesus offers (Jn 10:10).

WILLARD'S INTERPRETATION OF JESUS' BEATITUDES

The Sermon on the Mount is one of the central places of Scripture where Jesus addresses these great questions. In particular, Willard sees the Beatitudes as Jesus' answer to life's second great question, "Who is well-off?" While I almost always agree with Willard's approach to reading Scripture, of all his unique biblical interpretations, arguably the hardest to support is his commentary of the Beatitudes found in Matthew 5.[10] Given this, Gregg Ten Elshof, one of Willard's PhD students, offers a helpful perspective on the strengths and weaknesses of Willard's interpretation of the Beatitudes.

In contrast to the prevailing view of the Beatitudes—that they describe conditions people should pursue in order to be blessed (i.e., become "poor in spirit" in order to be blessed)—Willard states in *The Divine Conspiracy* that these teachings of Jesus cannot be "good news" if "they are understood as a set of 'how-tos' for achieving blessedness." Rather he writes, "They are explanations and illustrations drawn from the immediate setting, of the present availability of the kingdom through a personal relationship to Jesus."[11] He maintains that the Beatitudes provide proof that life with God is available in life circumstances that are beyond all human hope. They are descriptions of the kinds of people who, in their context, would have been categorized as hopeless.

As an example, Willard translates "the poor in spirit" in Matthew 5:3 by stating, "Blessed are the spiritually deprived, for they too find the kingdom of the heavens."[12] This translation emphasizes Willard's point that you should not seek to become "poor in spirit" in order to be blessed. Rather, people who are deprived spiritually are surprisingly well positioned to experience blessing, because the kingdom is near.

From this perspective, the Beatitudes are not meritorious conditions we should seek to achieve in order to become well-off. We should not strive to mourn, or to become meek, or to hunger and thirst for righteousness, or to be merciful or pure in heart, or to become peacemakers or persecuted. Instead, Willard says, "in spite of and in the midst of their ever so deplorable condition, the rule of the heavens has moved redemptively upon them by the grace of God."[13]

Here is where Ten Elshof finds difficulty with Willard's view. While he believes it makes good sense to say that someone can receive God's blessing *despite* their poverty or persecution or tragic circumstance, he does not believe it is as plausible to suggest to someone that they can still be blessed *in spite of* their purity of heart or peacemaking disposition.[14] Purity of heart and peacemaking are qualities that should not be viewed as undesirable life conditions, but as virtues. Thus, while Ten Elshof affirms Willard's view that the Beatitudes teach that blessing is available to all, because the kingdom of God is near, he believes we must leave behind the contention that Jesus accomplishes the goal of blessing others by "giving his audience a list of conditions *in spite of which* blessing could be theirs."[15]

Thankfully, Ten Elshof does not stop at critiquing Willard's interpretation of the mystery of the Beatitudes. Rather, he offers his interpretative solution to this text. He maintains that there are two unifying themes of the Beatitudes. First, he believes that none of the characteristics Jesus lists would "have been thought true of the Pharisees or the other members of the ruling religious class."[16] In other words, Jesus is proclaiming to his audience that you can be blessed without having to look and act like those leaders who think they are the only ones with the good life. Second, Ten Elshof adds that Jesus "cites a full spectrum of conditions in order to make clear to his audience that this is for *everyone*."[17] Given the wide-ranging variety of both virtues Jesus names and unfortunate conditions he includes, Jesus illustrates through the Beatitudes that the kingdom of God is available to all.

Overall, I believe Gregg Ten Elshof offers an important and necessary critique of Willard's view. Not only so, but I believe Ten Elshof contributes wonderful solutions to the dilemma of what links the unique themes of the Beatitudes together. From a personal standpoint, interpreting the Beatitudes as being *anti-Pharisee* in nature was a breakthrough insight for me. I believe this makes sense, because Jesus states in Matthew 5:20 (NIV), just a few verses after the Beatitudes: "For I tell you that unless your righteousness surpasses that of the Pharisees and the teachers of the law, you will certainly not enter the kingdom of heaven."

EXTENDED TRANSLATIONS

Another essential aspect of learning to read Scripture like Dallas Willard is to study his extensive translations of biblical passages. While Willard did not endeavor to craft his own equivalent to Eugene Peterson's *The Message* translation of Scripture, he nevertheless did a lot of Bible translating. Many of his personal Bible translations are published in his books, and he quoted them extensively in his teachings. For our purposes, let's examine two of these translations from the Sermon on the Mount: the Lord's Prayer, and Jesus' teaching on worry.

In *The Divine Conspiracy*, Willard reflects that he did not find the Lord's Prayer to be "the doorway into a praying life" until he reached his midtwenties. Like many of us, Dallas grew up engaging the Lord's Prayer—almost exclusively—by reciting it in unison. At some point, though, for reasons he could not explain, he began to use the prayer differently. He would take each phrase of the prayer and enter into the depths of its meaning in an unhurried, meditative fashion. Following the structure of this prayer, he would elaborate on Jesus' words—phrase by phrase—by drawing from the details of his everyday life.[18]

Building on this, Willard counsels that it may be beneficial to "reword the prayer to capture better the fullness of its meanings and its place in the gospel of the kingdom."[19] The following translation of the Lord's Prayer represents Dallas's personal experience with this treasured prayer.

> Dear Father always near us,
> may your name be treasured and loved,
> may your rule be completed in us—
> may your will be done here on earth
> in just the way it is done in heaven.
> Give us today the things we need today,
> and forgive us our sins and impositions on you
> as we are forgiving all who in any way offend us.
> Please don't put us through trials,
> but deliver us from everything bad.
> Because you are the one in charge,
> and you have all the power,
> and the glory too is all yours—forever—which is just
> the way we want it![20]

Following this, Willard adds what may be the most unique of all his biblical interpretations. He reflects, "Just the way we want it" is not a bad paraphrase for *amen*. But then he suggests another alternative to *amen*: "If your nerves can take it, you might (occasionally?) try 'Whoopee!' I imagine God himself will not mind."[21]

I'll let you decide for yourself if you want to finish your prayers with "Whoopee!" or not. I'll confess, this is one way I do *not* read Scripture like Dallas Willard, but I appreciate his humorous attempt to capture the spirit of *amen*.

While there's much that could be commented on in relation to Willard's translation, the primary thing I'd like to draw your attention to is its *realism*. Dallas begins by addressing God as being always near us.[22] As we discovered, when you pray to God, God comes right up to you. In Willard's translation, he corrects our notion that God is distanced from us when we pray, because he is, in fact, nearer to us than our very breath.

That changes how we pray. That changes how we ask God for what we need. That changes how we confess our sin, seek deliverance from evil, or intercede for others. This translation of the Lord's Prayer, then, is an example for how we should not only pray to God, but for how we should read his Word. Just as God as the author of Scripture never leaves his book alone, so God as the Creator never leaves his people alone. The Father is always near us.

Along with the Lord's Prayer, in *The Divine Conspiracy*, Willard also offers an in-depth translation of Matthew 6:25-34. It is from this context that Dallas makes one of his most controversial statements about the nature of God and the world we find ourselves in. "With this magnificent God positioned among us, Jesus brings assurance that our universe is a *perfectly safe place for us to be*."[23] What on earth could Dallas mean by this? Hasn't he seen the suffering of the world around us? Hasn't he personally experienced the painful losses of those he's loved? If Dallas was this smart, how could he be this naive, even insensitive to the suffering of others, to issue such a statement?

I believe Dallas could make such a bold claim as this because he really believed what Jesus taught about kingdom living. When we step into and live in the kingdom, things like worry and fear begin to fade away. No, that doesn't mean our circumstances are always going to turn out like we'd want. But we will be alive to a reality that transcends our daily concerns.

Here is a portion of Willard's translation of Matthew 6 that opens kingdom reality to us:

> My advice would be not to worry about what is going to happen to you. . . . Instead, make it a top priority to be part of what God is doing and to have the kind of goodness he has. Everything else you need will be provided.
>
> Tomorrow? Don't worry about it. You can do your worrying about tomorrow.[24]

Over the years, I've found so much freedom and hope through Willard's translation of Jesus' words. They remind me that living liberated from worry really is a possibility for apprentices of Jesus, as we keep the Lord always before us (Ps 16:8). For years, I've kept a printed-out translation of this passage in my Bible, in order to draw close to God and his kingdom when life's trials attempt to pull me into worry. As we keep a vision of God's never-ending world before us, by his grace, we can be freed from the strangling grip of worry.

These extended translations of Scripture from Willard reveal how we can practically read Scripture realistically and experientially. I can only imagine how much more peace and spiritual power the church would have if we engaged God's Word like Dallas did.

WILLARD WORDS

As a renowned philosopher, Dallas Willard spent significant time and effort defining words. For years, I kept a separate file of "Willard Words" to capture how Dallas defined many of the words Christians use—words they discover in the Bible without seriously considering what they mean. To read Scripture like

Dallas—especially the New Testament—it's essential for us to know how Dallas defined key words in Scripture and apply those definitions to specific passages where they're found. Let me offer you a couple examples of how I have found this to be fruitful.

Let's begin with the word *love*. According to Willard, "Love means will-to-good, willing the benefit of what or who is loved." In our culture, Willard notes, we have a great problem differentiating between love and desire, but it is essential we do so. We may say we *love* ice cream, but actually we only *desire* it, because our intent is to eat it. He writes, "New Testament Greek has several words for 'love.' Two are *eros* (from which we get 'erotic') and *agape*." To clarify the meaning of *agape*, Dallas says, "*Agape* love, perhaps the greatest contribution of Christ to human civilization, *wills the good of whatever it is directed upon*."[25]

Based on this definition of love, how might we best go about loving our neighbors as ourselves (Mt 22:39)? Oftentimes, we can mistakenly think that loving someone means doing everything they want you to do. Sometimes, though, someone might be asking you to do something that would not be for their ultimate good. When moments like these arise, we find ourselves in a dilemma. Do we do what the person wants us to do, or not? If love is about willing the good of another, then we can conclude that the more loving thing is to *not* do what they are asking. They might not *feel* loved by your response, but you can gently explain why the decision you've made is intended for their greater good.

Another Willard word that has shaped my reading of the New Testament is his definition of the word *lost*. In *Renovation of the Heart*, Willard defines lost to mean, "to be *out of place*, to be omitted." To this definition he adds, "Something that is lost is something that is not where it is supposed to be, and therefore it is not integrated into the life of the one to whom it belongs and to whom it is lost." Being lost, then, Willard claims, is a condition, not an outcome. "We're not lost because we are going to wind up in the wrong place. We are going to wind up in the wrong place because we are lost."[26] Being lost even impacts how we relate to ourselves. Dallas says, "When we are lost to God, we are also lost to ourselves: we do not know where we are or how to get where we want to go."[27]

Let's apply this definition of *lost* to a passage that is commonly referred to as Jesus' mission statement. In Luke 19:10 (NIV), he says, "The Son of Man came to seek and to save the lost." How might Willard's understanding shape how you interpret the word *lost* in this statement?

For me, I sense more compassion in Jesus' mission than I otherwise would have. The people Jesus refers to as lost are not just horrible, depraved people headed for hell, as I may have previously thought. Rather, Jesus is coming to save, teach, lead, and guide those who simply don't know where they are. Since they don't know *where* they are, they probably struggle to know *who* they are. Willard's understanding of being lost enables me to see greater compassion in Jesus' mission, and it challenges me to look at the lost in my life—including myself—more compassionately as well.

There are many more Willard words we could study, but by now, I hope my point has been made. To read Scripture like Dallas Willard, we must understand and apply Willard's well-reasoned definitions of central biblical words when we find them in the text. In the experiential exercises below, I provide you with an opportunity to practice this with the words *faith* and *joy*.

Throughout our journey, we have learned a significant number of ways we might read Scripture more like Dallas Willard did. Now, as we turn to our final chapter, let's imagine how we might *teach* Scripture like Dallas Willard taught it.

EXPERIENTIAL EXERCISES

1. Read through the Sermon on the Mount in Matthew 5–7. How does Jesus answer life's four great questions in this teaching?

2. Pray through the Lord's Prayer line by line, following both a traditional version of this prayer and Willard's translation. How do you resonate with Dallas's understanding of the Lord's Prayer? Where do you feel resistance to his understanding? Would you be bold enough to close your prayer by saying, "Whoopee!"?

3. Study the following passages of Scripture with the help of these Willard words:

   • In *Life Without Lack*, Dallas translates the word *faith* as "trust."[28] In *Renovation of the Heart*, Dallas says faith is "confidence grounded in reality."[29] Read the following passages by substituting the word *trust*, or the phrase "confidence grounded in reality," anytime you read the word *faith*: 2 Corinthians 5:7; Ephesians 2:8; Hebrews 11:1-6. How does Willard's understanding of faith shape your interpretation of these texts?

   • Dallas often said that "joy is a pervasive sense of well-being." In other words, even if everything might not be okay in your life, you can still be well-off, because God really is with you. Read the following passages while keeping this understanding of joy in mind: John 15:11; Romans 14:17; Hebrews 12:2. How does Dallas's definition of joy shape your understanding of these texts?

8

Teaching Scripture like Dallas Willard

*We must always remember, in hearing these words of Jesus
. . . that the art of the great teacher is to put things in ways
that you will remember even if you don't yet understand
them. In that way you can keep working on them (and they
on you) until you do understand them. Jesus is the master
teacher of the human race, and he teaches accordingly.*

DALLAS WILLARD, *RENOVATION OF THE HEART*

MY FAVORITE PREACHING BOOK IS *The Art & Craft of Biblical Preaching*, edited by legendary homiletics professor Haddon Robinson and pastor Craig Brian Larson. This work features over two hundred articles devoted to helping pastors and communicators of the gospel hone the craft of their calling.

Since I first read this book in 2005, one article has risen above the rest for its significance in shaping how I teach—week by week, year after year. This piece wasn't written by a preaching professor or someone with regular Sunday morning pulpit responsibilities. *The Art & Craft of Biblical Preaching* is my favorite book on communicating the biblical message because within its pages I first discovered a vision of preaching captured from the beloved words of Psalm 23. It's a short article called "A Cup Running Over." And I'm sure you can guess who it's written by.

Dallas Willard's "A Cup Running Over" makes a compelling case for why preachers must find deep satisfaction in Christ in order to communicate with joy and power. As a result of this article, the principle of *preaching from the overflow* has become my cornerstone rule for teaching that I have lived by for nearly twenty years as a pastor. Gratitude for this belongs not just to Dallas, but to the wisdom of Robinson and Larson, for their surprising inclusion of a philosophy professor from USC in their list of preaching voices.

But for anyone who has heard Dallas speak, you know he belongs. You know he has much to say to pastors about how they can best steward their sacred vocation. And you know Willard constantly raised the level of expectations for pastors to aspire toward. In fact, Willard boldly asserted that pastors are to be "teachers of the nations."[1]

Teachers of the nations? Seminary didn't exactly prepare me for that!

Through my years of learning to read Scripture like Dallas Willard, I've also paid careful attention to how I might teach Scripture like Dallas did. I'd venture to suggest that nearly any fruitfulness I have experienced as a communicator is a direct result of applying the pedagogical principles I've learned from Dallas over many years. To best organize and share what I've learned and practiced, I offer these ten Willard Ways for teaching Scripture.

WILLARD WAY ONE—SPEAK FROM THE OVERFLOW OF A SATISFIED SOUL

To teach Scripture like Dallas Willard, we must first read Scripture experientially. We must be with God ourselves before we can lead others into his presence. In "A Cup Running Over," Dallas describes how he learned to speak from the overflow of a satisfied soul in Christ:

> In my early days of ministry, I spent huge amounts of time absorbed in Scripture and the great spiritual writers. The Lord made it possible for me to spend whole days—without any issue of preparing for something or taking an examination—soaking up the Scripture. I literally wore out the books of great spiritual writers. This focus was foundational to my spiritual journey, to finding satisfaction in Christ. Experiencing God in that way leads me to satisfaction in Christ and to speaking to others out of that satisfaction. There is no substitute for simple satisfaction in the Word of God, in the presence of God. That affects all your actions.[2]

To find this satisfaction in Christ in Scripture, we must not settle for simply gaining insight from what God has communicated. Rather, we must move from hearing *communication* from God to enjoying *communion* with God. We must not seek the consolation prize of insight. We must pursue *encountering* God in the pages of his Word.

To do so, Willard recommends that we have substantial times every week when we do nothing but enjoy God.[3] This might include taking an unhurried walk or being fully present in the company of family and friends. And, yes, this involves enjoying the presence of God while we read and meditate and memorize his Word.

The most spiritually dynamic part of my sermon preparation each week happens on Saturday night. At this point, I have soaked myself in the text I'm preaching all week long (or longer) and sat with a completed manuscript that's been written for a couple days. I've organized slides to be shown during my sermon, and I've crafted small group questions. This is the point in my preparation commonly described as "internalizing the message." The goal is to be able to communicate the message conversationally, empowered by the Spirit, without being bogged down or distracted by my notes.

As I work through the different movements of my sermon, committing many of the key phrases to memory, I am also paying close attention to how God might be stirring my heart. His aim, overall, isn't just to help me prepare a message. He endeavors to transform me, as his messenger.

Almost without exception, through this prayerful period of preparation, God moves in some way that invites me to stop what I'm doing and encounter his presence. Sometimes God brings a memory to mind. Other times God convicts me of how *I* need to hear this message. But until this moment of communion with God occurs, I never feel fully ready to stand up and preach multiple services the next day. But after experiencing this moment of encounter, I know I am ready to preach from the overflow of my satisfied soul in Christ.

WILLARD WAY TWO—TEACH AS AN ACT OF LOVE, NOT AS A WAY TO IMPRESS

What are we hoping *overflows* when we teach? The power of God's loving presence. Freely we have received God's love, so naturally, we freely give God's love to others. Teaching is an opportunity to love our neighbors as ourselves. To love them, as we discovered earlier, is to will their good.

When we speak, our focus should not be on managing the impressions others have of us—how good we are, how dynamic we are, how spiritual we are. That would be willing *our* good, not our hearers' good. Preaching from the overflow of God's love frees us to be able to speak with humility.

Humility is what allows you to be realistic about who you are and who you're not. It's not the death *of* ourselves, but the death *to* ourselves—to our egoic operating systems.[4] When ego dies, God's power is given greater opportunity to work.

Willard frequently shared his three-step plan for humility:

1. Never pretend.

2. Never presume.

3. Never push.[5]

When we *pretend* to be someone we're not when we teach, we're giving the reins of our talk to the runaway ego. Ego says, "Impress." Humility says, "Love." If the end game of our Christian spiritual formation is to be pervaded with the *agape* love of Christ, then we must not give our egos any room to roam. Never pretend.

If we're never to manage the impressions we give to others by pretending, then we must never *presume* the people we teach should respond to us in a certain way. When we interact with others about our teaching—especially after we deliver a message—we should have no expectation about how they will treat us. When our souls are satisfied in Christ, we don't need to look to those we're called to serve to affirm our work.

Willard's third step for cultivating humility should be required for anyone teaching in Christ's name to agree to: *never push.* The most unpalatable preaching occurs when a speaker is trying too hard to make something happen. Pushing to be liked through nauseating, self-congratulatory storytelling. Pushing to conjure up heightened emotional responses by overly increasing volume of speech. Pushing people to change through guilt, shame, or manipulation.

How did Dallas Willard endeavor to preach lovingly through humility? Willard's friend Jan Johnson tells the story of the time she boldly asked Dallas after one of his classes, "So do you *try* not to be a good speaker?" Johnson wasn't attempting to be critical; she was just having a moment of awareness of Dallas's unique teaching methodology.

Dallas replied, "Yes, Jan, I just *go and talk to people*, and let God deal with them."[6] Why did Dallas do this? Because he had learned to ruthlessly eliminate impression management from his life. In the sacred interaction that occurs between speaker and hearers, there can be no pushing whatsoever.

In *Renovation of the Heart*, Willard challenges ministers to eliminate all performance from their work. He writes, "Performance is where we try to make an impression rather than just be what we are." To this he adds, "The minister does not need tricks and techniques, but need only speak Christ's word from Christ's character, standing within the manifest presence of God."[7] This, of course, should not happen exclusively in the context of sermon delivery. Speaking Christ's word from Christ's character is a calling to an overall lifestyle.

I believe Willard would say we should love our listeners by keeping them in mind when we speak. One way we can do this is by speaking as clearly and cogently as possible. Willard believes people are "desperate to hear something good. So clarify your thoughts by writing them out." Moreover, Willard insisted that we must be able "to say things with force and clarity." Writing out what we intend to say and teach "is one of the surest ways to hone your sense of what you're saying."[8] Love your listeners by preparing diligently. But never trust your preparation when you speak. Trust God.

As we do this, we should deliver our messages as *conversationally* as possible. We don't need to rush; we should give time for people to think. Dallas says, "Don't just rattle on. Literally pause."[9] Pausing allows space for the Creator to deal with his creatures, as Ignatius taught.

Test your own teaching motives for a moment. When have you taught as a way to impress? How might you—whenever you're given the opportunity to speak in Jesus' name—teach as an act of love? To teach Scripture like Dallas Willard, let *agape* overflow.

WILLARD WAY THREE—DISRUPT THE FLOW OF A HEARER'S LIFE

In *The Divine Conspiracy*, Willard writes, "The secret of the great teacher is to speak words, to foster experiences, that impact the active flow of the hearer's life. That is what Jesus did by the way he taught." The way Jesus taught, Willard believes, is how Jesus wants his disciples to teach others.[10]

In the course I took with Dallas, I watched him model this principle in several key ways. First, he shaped experiences that disrupted the normal flow and rhythm of our daily lives. Rather than have us enjoy lunch together, Willard invited us to follow his practice of fasting on Wednesday—using the time we would have spent in conversation around the dining tables to engage in silence and solitude.

All these years later, I can vividly recall how odd this experience felt. It didn't seem spiritually enlivening. It felt frustrating to have to be hungry and quiet and alone. Yet prior to that, the spiritual disciplines of silence, solitude, and fasting were virtually absent from my life. Now, they're an integral part of my relationship with God.

One of the ways I have attempted to practically disrupt the flow of my hearers' lives through teaching has been through the following exercise. Dallas often taught that we should remove automatic responses in our lives that are antithetical to God's kingdom.[11] The automatic response in my life that takes me away from the kingdom most is the perpetual distraction I experience from checking my phone too frequently. To assess whether or not I'm growing in this area, I regularly monitor my average daily screen time on my iPhone. Typically, I average around three hours a day. (But you should know, two and a half hours of that time are all spent on the Bible app memorizing Scripture! Eh, not quite.)

At this point in my talk, I'll invite the group to take out their phones and share—or better, *confess*—what their average daily screen time was for the week. The first time I did this, it was at an elite Christian preparatory academy outside of Boston. From all over the room, students started shouting out their daily average screen times. It was like an auction gone wild.

"Six hours!"

"Nine hours!"

The numbers kept climbing until an eighth-grade girl blurted out, "Thirteen hours!"

After that, the whole room let out a gasp, and it began to fall relatively silent. Not just this girl, but all of us somehow felt exposed. Implicated. There's something seriously wrong with the patterns of our world when a Christian middle schooler, from an elite academy, is spending more than half of her day staring at the screen of her phone. But it's not just her. It's all of us. We've all contributed to this distracted state of affairs. To invite people into an eternal kind of life today, we have to show them just how *off* our *normal* way of doing things is.

Not only did Dallas believe we should disrupt the flow of a hearer's life through curated experiences, but by correcting the prevailing assumptions of the culture. Throughout Willard's body of work, he speaks repeatedly of how our culture has deteriorated through what he calls "the disappearance of moral knowledge."[12]

He writes in *Knowing Christ Today*:

> To say that moral knowledge has disappeared is just to say that what those people knew, and know now, is *no longer made available to the public as knowledge by the institutions of knowledge in our social and political system*, though it was made available at times in the past.[13]

The result of this disappearance is the relegation of moral knowledge to the domains of subjective feeling and cultural tradition.[14]

I raise this point not to get into a lengthy discussion about this topic, but to demonstrate one of Willard's key teaching philosophies. We must correct the prevailing assumptions of our culture that run counter to the way of Jesus as taught in Scripture. To do this, we must be students of our cultural moment, and be aware of what Willard describes as people's "mental furniture"—what they give their thoughts and attention to.[15] "The satisfied preacher," Willard writes, "speaks from a listening heart. Since people often do not know what they really need, such preaching can help them find out."[16]

To preach as a wonderfully disruptive teacher—as Dallas was—we must devote our lives to listening well. To listening to and understanding culture. And to listening as an act of love to the people to whom we are called to minister.

WILLARD WAY FOUR—GIVE 'EM HEAVEN

If you've ever been in a locker room, about to take the field before a big game, chances are you've likely heard a coach say something to the effect of "Give 'em hell." That advice has oddly seemed to translate to the Christian pulpit. Early in my ministry training, I remember hearing the adage, "You've got to get people lost before you can get people found." In other words, to help people want the good life in Christ, you first have to show them just how bad they are.

In classic fashion, Dallas turned this common phrase, "Give 'em hell," into what has become another "Dallas-ism": *Give 'em heaven!* By this Dallas meant to "preach what Jesus preached in the manner Jesus preached it."[17] What did Jesus come proclaiming? The kingdom of God is available. An eternal kind of life is possible now. Through not just our message, but through our very way of being, we as teachers must extend this grand invitation—life's greatest opportunity—every time we communicate.

The importance of this point is captured best through the reflections of Dallas's granddaughter, Larissa Heatley:

> I will always remember one sentence that really summed up everything he stood for and everything I need to do.

He might not have meant it as anything, but I kept thinking about it. He said it to me in the hospital just before his last surgery. We were all walking out of the room and I was about to go to sing with my youth choir at a homeless shelter. Grandpa called me back for a moment so we were the only two in the room, and he said, "Give 'em heaven." At that time I'm pretty sure he just meant it as a joke—or maybe he didn't. He had a way of saying something so meaningful without really knowing it. So anyway, "Give 'em heaven." That is what I plan to do.[18]

And to teach Scripture like Dallas Willard, that's what we must do too: *Give 'em heaven.*

WILLARD WAY FIVE—LEVERAGE
THE POWER OF VIM

How did Dallas Willard structure his teachings? Often in his lectures he provided students with a dense outline to follow, filled with extensive quotations from Scripture and other writings. But beyond that, was there an overall pattern he followed to give shape to his teachings? In some of the messages I've heard Dallas deliver, his presentation felt less like a clearly structured keynote address, and more like an easygoing conversation taking place among friends along a leisurely walk.

Beyond the conversational tone and flow of many of Dallas's teachings, there was an underlying, implicit structure he followed. This is best expressed through what Dallas calls the reliable pattern for how God changes lives—the little acronym VIM, which stands for *vision, intention,* and *means.*[19]

In *Renovation of the Heart,* Dallas demonstrates how real-life change occurs as people first capture a *vision* of life in the kingdom. This is almost assuredly why saying, "Give 'em heaven" carries so much meaning. Without a picture—not just of a preferable *future* (as vision is often described), but also of a preferable *present*—people rarely change. For this reason, Dallas often began his messages by casting a vision for what would be possible if we chose life as an apprentice in Jesus' kingdom.

For life change to occur, an *intention* for this vision to be enacted must be made through a deliberate decision. When listening to Dallas, I often heard him gently nudge his hearers to be people who intend to do everything Jesus said. He would offer invitations for people to decide to become the kind of person who would more easily and routinely do everything Jesus said. In structuring and delivering messages, Dallas very intuitively leveraged the power of intention—inviting people to enroll in Jesus' master class of life.

Finally, Willard pointed people to the *means* by which we might experience the vision of the kingdom as reality. Most often, these means included the spiritual disciplines of the Christian life—both disciplines of engagement and disciplines of abstinence. Willard never issued a call for people to simply *try* harder to live a more Christlike life. Rather, he invited people to *train* themselves to become the kind of people who more easily and routinely experience the power and joy of kingdom living.

One of the most succinct examples I have found of how Willard structured his teachings—following the pattern of VIM—is an article titled "How to Love Your Neighbor as Yourself," found in *Renewing the Christian Mind*, edited by Gary Black Jr.

Willard begins this teaching by communicating the vision that Jesus' command to love our neighbors as ourselves is something we can actually do. He writes, "We want to find a realistic understanding that loving our neighbor is something we can do in our actual world, in our real circumstances."[20] Willard then outlines the biblical basis for such a vision, focusing primarily on the Good Samaritan story found in Luke 10:29-37.

From this story, Willard states that neighborly love is founded on compassion. And "a person of compassion is one who feels the needs of others and whose compassion is not something that can be turned on and off like a water faucet." Willard then describes where the source of such compassion can be found. "We can 'afford' to be compassionate only if we know there is abundant compassion for us, toward us, by persons who have appropriate means."[21] This source, of course, is God, whose perfect love casts out fear.

Willard then observes the role fear plays in the Good Samaritan story. As a solution to this perennial neighboring problem, he asserts, "So, our experience of God's love is what allows us, empowers us, to set aside anger, selfishness, lusting, and so on in our relationships with others."[22] Outside of the dominating control of fear, genuine neighborly love becomes possible.

From this *vision*, he then invites his listeners to *intend* to become the kind of people who embody this neighborly love in their actual lives and present circumstances. To do so he says, "The first major step in becoming one of those who love their neighbors as themselves is to decide to live in compassion. Now let us be clear: this is a decision to receive the abundance of the kingdom of the heavens as the basis of your life."[23] Along with this decision to be compassionate, Willard states that we must decide who our neighbors are by making a list of people in terms of degrees of closeness.

Once these intentions are expressed through actual decisions, Willard offers three primary *means* by which we may grow in loving our neighbors as ourselves. First he says, "Begin to practice loving those closest to you, paying special attention to your sincere concern, assistance, and compassion for their lives through your words and action directed to those individuals. . . . Slowly work your way to your larger spheres of influence." Finally, he says, "Engage in the spiritual disciplines that enable you to operate from a constant fullness of grace."[24] What a phrase and power to live by—"a constant fullness of grace."

This teaching, "How to Love Your Neighbor as Yourself," is an explicit example of the structure Willard seems to implicitly implement whenever he delivers a message: vision, intention, means. It should not come as a surprise to us that the reliable pattern Willard believed God uses to change lives is the same pattern he often followed in structuring his messages. How might your next teaching be strengthened by building it around VIM?

WILLARD WAY SIX—GREAT TEACHERS REPEAT THEMSELVES

It's been commonly understood that repetition is the mother of all learning. Based on Dallas's books, teachings, and lectures, I'd venture to suggest this was a principle he embraced, because Dallas repeated himself. A lot.

Some of the key themes that appear in almost all of Dallas's books include definitions of words like *kingdom*, *grace*, and *love*. Dallas often included central themes to his ministry in many books and articles, like the spiritual disciplines and the four great questions. I'll confess that at times, while reading Willard, I've had moments where I'd kind of roll my eyes at how repetitive he could be. I'd arrogantly think, "He's getting as much mileage as he can out of this point." But I think this says more about me than it does about Dallas.

I wonder why many preacher types like me can be resistant to being viewed as repetitive? Do we fear appearing ignorant of our past teachings or of being underprepared? Are we too worried about coming across as boring to our congregations? Maybe our resistance to repetition has more to do with our preoccupation toward image management and less to do with love? Or do we resist teaching through repetition because we have lost our attention spans for learning through repetition ourselves?

No matter why we resist repetition, we must examine how effective our series-to-series, on-to-the-next-thing ministry philosophies and discipleship approaches really are. I'm quite certain Dallas chose to be repetitive *intentionally*, not *accidentally*. Just because we *say it*, doesn't mean others *get it*. In our day and age of reduced church engagement, it's time we abandon our fears of being seen as repetitive.

Let us embrace repetition as a key practice for teaching people to do everything Jesus said. Dallas did. And so did Jesus. Consider how many times he started a lesson with the idea: "The kingdom is like . . ." Repetition was a hallmark of Willard's teaching, because it was central to Jesus' way of making disciples. Great teachers repeat themselves.

WILLARD WAY SEVEN—GO WITH THOSE WHO GO

In my pastoral experience, I've found people gravitate far more to talking about discipleship than to actually living as Jesus' disciples. Attempting to successfully "teach people to do everything" Jesus commanded can feel deeply discouraging, so we often just skip that step—what Willard referred to as the Great Omission in the Great Commission.

During a break in one of my doctoral courses, I asked my instructor, Trevor Hudson, what his experience was like attempting to make disciples within his South African church context. He said his experience was very similar to mine. A lot of people begin the discipleship journey, but few continue it. Then he shared the advice Willard gave to him when Hudson expressed similar frustrations about making disciples. "Go with those who go," Dallas said.

To teach Scripture like Dallas Willard, we need to pay attention to the primary groups Dallas taught. Most frequently Dallas spoke to groups of forty people or less. This included decades of Sunday school teaching, doctor of ministry courses at Fuller Theological Seminary, and instruction through the Renovaré Institute. Only rarely did he speak to crowds of thousands. I believe the reason for this wasn't because of a lack of opportunity, but because of his intentional discipleship strategy. I think Dallas would agree that teaching people to live as Jesus' disciples happens far better in smaller, more intimate settings, than from large platforms on the biggest conference stages.[25] But even though the classroom might not look as attractive as the stage, you never know when you might have someone sitting in your Sunday school course who turns out to be Richard Foster.[26]

To *go with those who go*, teachers of Scripture must arrange their overall working lives so that they can devote significant time to teaching people in smaller, more intimate and conversational settings. If *more is caught than taught*, as educational theory often suggests, than to teach Scripture like Dallas Willard did, we must make ourselves both available and vulnerable to others. That kind of genuine availability and vulnerability can't happen from the big stage, like it can over a meal. But the stage can be a way for inviting people who are interested in "going" to go even deeper in a more intimate environment.

At the church I serve, I developed a more intentional spiritual formation environment to *go with those who are going* in our congregation. It's called Monday school. It's designed to offer interactive teaching and learning experiences through small group conversation, integration of spiritual practice, and question-and-answer opportunities, which accompany a shorter teaching that will frame our time together.

To pull this off, I have to devote less time to preparing the most polished Sunday sermon I can. Yet I'd suggest my Sunday teaching has been strengthened by all of my Monday interactions with people grappling with how to *go*. What happens Monday has profoundly shaped the culture of Sunday. Church is less *attractional* in its model, but more *attractive* because of its formation focus.

To go with those who go, think *go deeper with few*, rather than *reach wider with many*. Then watch and wait. The depth will increase the breadth. And just to be clear, Dallas didn't exactly invent this church strategy either. I think Jesus did. And I'd say it turned out pretty well.

WILLARD WAY EIGHT—EVALUATE: IS MY TEACHING HAVING THE NATURAL RESULT OF MAKING DISCIPLES?

Dallas Willard insisted that the gospel *we're* preaching should be the same gospel *Jesus* preached. In order to assess not just *how* we're teaching the gospel but *if* we're preaching the gospel Jesus preached, Dallas declared that all who speak for Christ must constantly ask themselves: "Does the gospel I preach and teach have a natural tendency to cause people who hear it to become full-time students of Jesus?"[27] If the answer is almost exclusively no, then we must step back and truly consider if our teaching is making disciples or consumers of religious goods and services. While no one will ever have a perfect track record of making disciples when they preach—Jesus didn't—we should take time with regularity, and with the help of this penetrating question, to assess our effectiveness of preaching the gospel.

Along with this evaluative question, Dallas also recommended that pastors and teachers of Scripture listen to their critics. In "Becoming the Kind of Leaders Who Can Do the Job," he writes:

> Listen to your critics. . . . Listen not with the attitude "I don't deserve this, they're dead wrong." Lay it down and just listen; see what you can learn. Practice walking off without reply. What goes along with this is: don't defend yourself . . . you have a defender, and you let him do his job.[28]

Criticism might be the unwanted raw material God wants to use to help you become more whole and more holy—and more effective in your communication. Evaluate and listen."

WILLARD WAY NINE—LET GO OF THE OUTCOME

I remember John Ortberg once describing what it was like being with Dallas just after he gave a talk at a significant conference. Rather than seeing Dallas concerned with how he did, or what people thought, John said being with Dallas was like watching a little child let go of a helium balloon outside. Dallas released his teaching into the loving arms of his Savior, almost without a care in the world. How could Dallas do this? He learned to let go of the outcome of his ministry and relinquish it to God.

In *Renovation of the Heart*, Dallas emphasizes the importance of "abandoning outcomes."[29] To do this, we acknowledge and accept that we do not have the capacity or wherewithal to make a situation come out right, regardless of what that situation is. This acceptance of our finitude and limits is a crucial part of what it means to be humble. According to Willard, "Humility is the great secret of rest of soul because it does not presume to secure outcomes."[30]

I believe Dallas discovered an important insight like this through one of his many encounters with God. In "A Cup Running Over," Dallas describes a powerful moment he shared with God as he was about to begin preaching. "One of my great joys came when I got up from a chair to walk to the podium and the Lord said to me, 'Now remember, it's what I do with the Word between your lips and their hearts that matters.'"[31]

If what God does—in the moment between speaking and hearing—is what matters most, then we can trust him enough to let go of the outcome of our teaching, like a child letting go of a helium balloon into the open sky. Maybe abandoning outcomes is what childlike faith, or maybe even childlike preaching, looks like.

WILLARD WAY TEN—NEVER TRY TO FIND A PLACE TO SPEAK; TRY TO HAVE SOMETHING TO SAY

In 2003, during a luncheon at the C. S. Lewis Foundation Summer Conference, Dallas reflected on a pivotal point in his vocational journey, which helped to shape his path to tenure at a secular university.

> I'm afraid to say this, because I'm afraid to burden someone else. But I never ask for a promotion. I never ask for money. Of the books I've published, all have been solicited from me by the publishers. And I'll tell you why I have approached things in this way. When I was at Baylor University as a young man, as a very green young man, I was watching other green young men trying to find a place to preach. And the Lord said something very simple to me: "Never try to find a place to speak, try to have something to say." If you read my books, you know that I really do believe the Lord speaks to us. And one reason I believe the Lord speaks to me is because I don't have enough sense to know things like that. So that helped me a lot, just in terms of what I don't have to mess with and what I then can concentrate on.[32]

Don't try to find a place to speak. Become the kind of person who has something to say. I love these words, and the more I've lived by them, the more freedom I've felt, and the more my trust in God has deepened. When we communicate from the overflow of our satisfied soul, we'll be people who have something to say. And if we are people who have something to say, we can trust that God will provide us with opportunities to speak.

In another address, Dallas gives the following advice to people who are looking to find their place in this world: "Don't strive to advance yourself. Let God advance you."[33] As a young, restless preacher, there were definitely times I didn't think God was advancing me at the rate I thought he should. But over time, God has blessed me with the grace to grow in patience toward him.

Letting God advance you is not a prescription for passive living. It is a corrective to the overreaching ambition that taints the motivations of too many ministers—including me. When I let God advance me, I can more faithfully serve *today* as I actively wait for God's leading *tomorrow.*

Read Scripture like Dallas Willard did. Preach from the overflow of a satisfied soul. Listen lovingly. And you will become a person who has something to say.

When God gives you a place to speak, *Give 'em heaven!*

EXPERIENTIAL EXERCISES

1. Watch one of Dallas's most accessible and most viewed online teachings, "Life in the Spirit," from a Wheaton College chapel service in 2009.[34] Notice how he speaks from the overflow of a satisfied soul. Pay attention to the various ways he attempts to lovingly disrupt the flow of

his hearers' lives through the questions he raises. Consider how he attempts to give these students the kingdom of heaven. Witness the freedom with which Dallas speaks— seeming to let go of the outcome of this message as he does so. How might Dallas's example shape the way you teach or communicate?

2. Which of these ten Willard Ways for teaching Scripture like Dallas Willard attracts you the most and why? Which would be most difficult to integrate into your life, ministry, or communication, and why?

3. Prepare your next teaching, Bible study, or sermon following these Willard Ways as closely as you can.

Conclusion

We'll See

*If you dwell in my word, you are really my
apprentices. And you will know the truth, and
the truth will liberate you. (John 8:31-32)*

DALLAS WILLARD'S TRANSLATION,
THE DIVINE CONSPIRACY

AFTER DALLAS DELIVERED A MESSAGE at a large pastors'
conference, one of his friends asked him how he thought his
talk went. Dallas replied, "We'll see."

For Willard, a presentation's success was not determined by
how well it was delivered or how well it was liked. The quality
of a teaching can only be determined through time—by how
much or how little of what was shared by the speaker is applied
in the lives of the hearers. The ministry of teaching, therefore,
goes well beyond what a communicator does. The ministry of
teaching is dependent on the ultimate teacher Jesus has given
us: the Holy Spirit.

Throughout this book, I have done my best to distill years of
learning to read Scripture like Dallas Willard into an accessible,
practical, and applicable Bible-reading approach that anyone

who has enrolled in Jesus' master class of life can incorporate into their own life. My hope: that you might have deeper experiences with God through Scripture, like Dallas and many of his spiritual influences did. Spiritual transformation occurs through experiential encounters in the presence of God.

While I'm grateful that you have made your way through the contents of this book, I hope its conclusion does not become the end of its practice in your life. My prayer is that this work becomes a resource that—like a faithful spiritual guide or friend—you turn to for many seasons to come. Nearly all of the ideas highlighted in this book took years for me to better understand, learn to apply, and experience the fruit of the effort invested. So let me encourage you to be patient.

According to Dallas, patience is "the willingness to let the life you're living grow and take the wise course."[1] Interacting with Scripture as *communication* that leads to *communion* necessitates a deep trust in the slow, unhurried work of God. Allowing *communion* to lead to *union* with God is the journey of our lifetime. So keep showing up expectantly. Relinquish your agenda. And enjoy the deep contentment, joy, and confidence that come from being with God in his Word.

LIFELONG LEARNING FROM DALLAS

I am often asked where someone should begin reading Dallas Willard. Typically, my response depends on the person who's asking. For someone who's never read Dallas before, I recommend *The Great Omission* or *Life Without Lack*. For readers who have made their way through this book, I'd recommend reading Willard's books following the flow of his four critical commitments.

To begin, read *The Divine Conspiracy*—the most important of Willard's works in my mind—which is devoted to the theme of robust metaphysical realism. Then read *The Spirit of the Disciplines*, followed by *Hearing God*. These works are dedicated to Willard's second critical commitment, epistemic realism. *Renovation of the Heart* focuses on Willard's third critical commitment, complete anthropology. Then read *Knowing Christ Today*, which highlights elements of Willard's last commitment, authentic change—leading to spiritual formation as a domain of public knowledge. Finally, read everything else Dallas wrote, including posthumously released works like *The Allure of Gentleness*.

Along with reading Dallas's books, watch and listen to him teach. Gary W. Moon and the team at Conversatio Divina (https://conversatio.org) have curated an extensive collection of audio and video recordings of Dallas over his ministry career. I would recommend watching the 2010 Denver Seminary course I took, which is included among the collection.[2] Along with this, I'd strongly suggest Willard's Spirituality and Ministry course, filmed in 2012.[3] There are many more teachings to learn from, but these would be my recommendations to get started.

Additionally, Dallas Willard Ministries continues to make more of Dallas's expansive ministry resources available at https://dwillard.org. I'm particularly grateful for Dallas's personal list of recommended books to read, which can be found on this site.[4] This list includes many of the sources that shaped how Dallas learned to read Scripture experientially, including *Deeper Experiences of Famous Christians* by James Gilchrist Lawson.

A TIME FOR EXPERIENTIAL
KNOWLEDGE OF GOD

Over the past few years, I've taught aspects of this curriculum to hundreds of pastors and ministry leaders in New England. Each time, someone comes up to me afterward and asks if I think experientially knowing God through Scripture could be the next wave of what God might do in the church. Although I'm no futurist, part of the reason I wrote this book is to help support the church if this new experiential movement of God were to occur. I believe we may be feeling the winds of what could incite a new wave of God's movement for this reason.

Wesley's famous quadrilateral asserted that there are four key ways that people determine what is real and true: Scripture, tradition, reason, and experience. Scripture is to be the norm that norms all norms, as the Reformers famously said. But over the past five hundred years (probably beyond that), it seems that something other than Scripture fights to become our ultimate source of knowledge.

In the decades leading up to the Reformation, church *tradition* seemed to triumph over Scripture as the ultimate authority guiding God's people. This led Reformers like Luther, Calvin, and others to call the church back to Scripture. During the period of the Enlightenment, *reason* triumphed over Scripture as people's ultimate authority. Now in our late modern or postmodern period, it appears our subjective human *experiences* have supplanted not only reason as a greater authority, but also Scripture. This seems to be true even among a growing number of Christians. The expressive individualism of our culture is shaping believers to such a degree that if our personal experiences appear to collide with what Scripture says, we are choosing to listen to what our experience tells us over Scripture. My hope and prayer is that Willard's experiential approach to reading Scripture might serve as a radical antidote. While our experiences significantly matter, they must remain tethered to the unchanging truth of Scripture. Yet Scripture is not just a set of propositions to follow. It's an invitation to grow in an ever-deepening relationship with God. May the recovery of an experiential approach to reading Scripture usher in a new way for people in our experiential age to encounter the presence of our eternal God.

A GIFT TO RECEIVE

Before my family left the Willard home during our visit in June 2023, Jane wanted to bless each of my children with a parting gift. While Jane had given many of Dallas's personal items to the Willard Archives at Westmont College, she held on to several items for occasions like these. She presented lovely gifts to my two younger children, but the gift she gave to our oldest, Dallas Ripper, was most meaningful.

She presented my son, Dallas, with a cross made out of olive wood from the Garden of Gethsemane that the Willards purchased while traveling to Israel in the 1980s. An absolutely extraordinary blessing for my family to receive.

While she was describing and presenting this gift to my Dallas, he simply opened up his hands, waiting to receive this gift. I've watched Dallas receive many gifts, and as a seven-year-old, he typically receives by grabbing or impatiently taking the gift being handed to him. But not this time.

Deeply moved by what he did, I quickly pulled him aside and asked him why he opened up his hands to receive the gift. He said something to this effect:

> Dad, this day has been a lot for me. Being in your hero's home, being with his wife, and being given this gift. I don't fully understand why this gift is so important, but I know it is. And I know I don't really deserve this gift either. So I just felt like I should open up my hands to receive it.

As I've reflected on that moment many times (often in tears), I'm struck with the reminder that every day a cross from Jesus *is* being extended to us. It's beyond what we could fully fathom. It's so much greater than anything we could ever deserve. Yet it's being given to us by God's grace as a gift to receive. All we can do is simply open up our hands like Dallas Ripper did.

Like the gift of the cross, reading Scripture experientially—like Dallas Willard read it—is a gift of grace. We can position ourselves as best as possible to encounter God, but the gift of his presence comes only from him. May we keep seeking him with open hands and trust the experiences will come.

Acknowledgments

THANKS TO DALLAS WILLARD, the unassuming, often-overlooked preposition *with* has found a place of prominence in my spiritual vocabulary. I do not simply live *for* God, I'm invited to live *with* God. As I live with God, the Lord surrounds me with wonderful people to serve with, play with, work with, live the with-God life with, and even write with. Without these friends, teachers, and fellow disciples of Jesus, this project never would have come to life.

Thank you, Gary W. Moon, for your unwavering encouragement from conception to completion of this book. The academic and spiritual setting you curated—along with the wonderful faculty, staff, and students of the Fuller Theological Seminary Doctor of Ministry in Spiritual Direction cohort—helped me gain the *experiential* knowledge needed for this endeavor. Thank you for confirming the necessity of this project and affirming your belief that I was the person to do it. I'm so grateful you blessed this project with your generous and inspiring foreword.

Thank you, Howard Baker. Since first meeting you at a Denver Seminary campus visit in 2006, you have been a constant example to me of what a Christlike, with-God, kingdom life is like. Thanks for making possible the opportunity to directly study with Dallas in 2010. Thank you for encouraging me to pursue this doctoral program, leading me through the Ignatian Exercises, and for journeying alongside me during every stage of writing. I would not be who I am personally or vocationally apart from your ongoing friendship.

Thank you, Trevor Hudson, for steering the trajectory of my spiritual life away from merely seeking insight, to pursuing spiritual encounter. I'm enjoying the "grand prize" more than ever before. Thank you for helping me discover the connections between Ignatius and Dallas, and for providing valuable guidance as I crafted this project.

Many thanks to the lovely Jane Willard. The way you've opened your home and life to my family is a gift we will treasure forever. Thanks for your encouragement and support of this project. Many thanks as well to the Willard Family Trust for extending so much time and energy toward ensuring this book best represents Dallas's life and work through your collective editorial guidance. A special thanks belongs to Dallas's daughter, Becky Willard Heatley, for graciously interacting with me throughout the editing stages of this project, and for your wonderful facilitation of the Dallas Willard Is My Homeboy Facebook group. (Yes, this really exists. Come join!) I'm so grateful for the connections I've been blessed to make through this group and for how my understanding of Dallas's ideas have deepened through your ongoing work.

Thank you, Al Hsu, and the entire editorial team at Inter-Varsity Press for your support of this book and for your commitment to producing thoughtful and beautiful kingdom-building resources. Extended thanks to you, Al, for your constant encouragement, wise guidance, and spiritual friendship through every high and low of this writing endeavor. I'm grateful for how you helped me cut a lot of clutter not only from this manuscript but also from my life. (You should have seen how much longer the previous sentence originally looked!)

Thank you to the leaders and congregation of Crossway Christian Church for your support of my doctoral program and this project. Thanks as well to all of the Monday School students who experienced version 1.0 of this curriculum and whose questions, reflections, and enthusiasm enhanced it significantly. It is such a privilege being one of your pastors.

To Charles Galda and Vision New England, for providing me with an abundance of opportunities to share this curriculum with leaders throughout our region. To the Melder family, for your friendship and for generously opening your beautiful mountain home to me, which served as a sacred space to write with God.

Thank you to my family for making so many sacrifices so I could complete this book. Thank you to grandparents for their support in helping to watch our kids while I spent time away to study and write. Thank you to my children, Dallas, Clive, and Avila, for helping me to find God in all the ordinary moments of life. I love you and look forward to seeing you experience the presence of God as you learn to read Scripture like Dallas Willard.

To my beautiful wife, Erin, whose wisdom, support, friendship, and pursuit of God make every part of my life—including this book—so much better. Thank you for reading every word I've written and every word I've rewritten, and rewritten again. Living in our God-bathed world with you is the greatest joy of my life. I love you and thank God for you.

And thank you, Lord, for the countless moments I felt carried along by your Spirit throughout this endeavor. The experiences we shared together throughout this writing process made every hurdle and every struggle more than worth it. I pray those who read this book experience your presence as I did while writing this book. Thank you for the good news of the gospel of the kingdom, as proclaimed in Scripture, which makes life with you possible now, and forever.

For God's greater glory, Amen.

Appendix

SUMMARY OF DALLAS WILLARD'S
SCRIPTURE-READING DISTINCTIVES

1. Learn Under the Ministry of Gifted Teachers	Dallas encouraged his students to find gifted teachers of Scripture and the spiritual life to learn from. Ask the Lord that he would provide people—like Dallas—who can guide you to experience God in Scripture and make you capable of studying fruitfully on your own.
2. Inerrant and Infallible	Willard believed the Bible is one of the ways God speaks to us. It is his unique written Word, inerrant in its original form and infallible in all of its forms—designed to lead his people toward kingdom living. God never leaves his Word alone, which is why it is authoritative and fully trustworthy.
3. The Bible Fixes the Boundaries of What God Will Say in Principle	In *Hearing God*, Dallas writes, "The Bible is a finite, written record of the saving truth spoken by the infinite, living God, and it reliably fixes the boundaries of everything he will ever say to humankind. It fixes those boundaries *in principle*, though it does not provide the detailed communications that God may have with individual believers today."[1]
4. Human and Divine Sides of the Bible	Dallas affirmed that there is a human side and a divine side to the Bible. On the human side, God used competent people to accurately shape and preserve the message of the Scripture in the context of their language, culture, and community. On the divine side, God preserved the written record and arrangement of his Word so his purpose and intention for humanity would be known.
5. The Bible Is God's Gift to the World	God did not give the Bible to a group of scholars. He gave the Bible to the church. The Bible, then, is not designed for mere academic study; it is a book to be lived. It necessitates a reading approach that is straightforward, rigorous, contextual, and thoughtful.
6. A Biblical Christian	Biblical Christians are not those who have high views about the Bible. Biblical Christians are those who intend to live eternal kinds of lives with God, as displayed in the pages of Scripture.
7. Reading Scripture Realistically	We should not read the Bible as if was about different kinds of people, in different kinds of places, in radically different times. Rather, the Bible is about us. We must make the resolute effort to believe what happened in the Bible could and should happen to people like us. We must imagine what it would be like if this were the case as we read. Willard's advocacy of biblical realism and affirmation of our participation in biblical experience is an example of how he read the Bible philosophically.

8. The Loss of Biblical Realism	Willard believed the dominant ideology of modern psychological thought is one of the most potent factors that has led to the demise of biblical realism. It has had the tendency to blunt or altogether undermine the realism of biblical language about the human self. Many streams of modern, secular psychological thought deny the reality or possibility of religious experience because it is not empirically verifiable.
9. Communication to Communion to Union	In *Hearing God*, Dallas offers his most straightforward definition of what the Bible is. "Scripture is a *communication* that establishes *communion* and opens the way to *union*, all in a way that is perfectly understandable once we begin to have experience of it."[2]
10. Knowledge by Acquaintance	There are three key ways of knowing someone or something: (1) propositional knowledge, (2) know-how, (3) knowledge by acquaintance. Willard's approach to reading the Bible involves all three forms of knowing, with particular emphasis on knowledge by acquaintance—knowing God personally, experientially, interactively.
11. The With-God Life	The integrative motif of the Bible, according to Willard, is the with-God life. The message from Genesis to Revelation is that God desires to live life with us. Dallas framed this idea by stating, "The aim of God in history is the creation of an all-inclusive community of loving persons with God himself at the very center of this community as its prime Sustainer and most glorious Inhabitant (Eph 2:19-22; 3:10)."[3]
12. Fifteen Movements of the With-God Life	(1) The People of God in Individual Communion; (2) The People of God Become a Family; (3) The People of God in Exodus; (4) The People of God in the Promised Land; (5) The People of God as a Nation; (6) The People of God in Travail; (7) The People of God in Prayer and Worship; (8) The People of God in Daily Life; (9) The People of God in Rebellion; (10) The People of God in Exile; (11) The People of God in Restoration; (12) The People of God with Immanuel; (13) The People of God in Mission; (14) The People of God in Community; (15) The People of God into Eternity[4]
13. Reading with a Submissive Attitude	To read the Bible realistically, we must read with a submissive attitude. Submissive reading entails reading "with a readiness to surrender all you are—all your plans, opinions, possessions, positions." This does not negate rigorous study of the Word; rather, we should "study as intelligently as possible, with all available means, but never study merely to find the truth and especially not just to prove something. Subordinate your desire to *find* the truth to your desire to *do* it, to act it out!"[5]
14. Getting the Bible Through Us	Willard warns against trying to read too much of the Bible at once. We are not to simply get through the Bible. Our goal is to get the Bible through us.

15. Approaching the Bible to Meet God	Scripture must be read expectantly. We should come to our selected text like we're going to a sacred place to meet with God.
16. Adaptation of *Lectio Divina*	The ancient practice of *lectio divina*, or sacred reading, involves five steps for Willard: (1) *information*, (2) *longing* for it to be so, (3) *affirmation* that it *must* be so, (4) *invocation* to make it so, (5) *appropriation* by God's grace that it *is* so.[6]
17. Reading with an Ignatian Imagination	Imagination is an avenue, not an obstacle to engaging God in Scripture. Like Ignatius taught, we must boldly and prayerfully employ our imagination as we read the stories of people who met with God.
18. Keeping Company with Jesus in the Gospels	The Gospels must become an essential part of our daily diet of Scripture. We should take the next decades to read and meditate on Matthew, Mark, Luke, and John, until we have encountered Christ personally through the events, teachings, and stories of these books of the Bible.
19. Memorize Scripture as You Can, not as You Can't	Bible memorization was the single most important spiritual discipline in Dallas Willard's life. To read the Bible like he did, we must consistently commit God's Word to memory—internalizing it in our hearts. Then all of our lives can become a quiet time.
20. You Have to Dig	Dallas believed the Bible was the most profound book in human history—by far. Because of its depth, we must dig deeply into it by studying it, memorizing it, and living it. Through in-depth engagement with the text, the richness of Scripture is revealed.

[1]Dallas Willard, *Hearing God: Developing a Conversational Relationship with God* (Downers Grove, IL: InterVarsity Press, 1999), 142–43.

[2]Willard, *Hearing God*, 161.

[3]Richard Foster et al., eds., *The Life with God Bible* (New York: Harper Collins, 2005), xxvii.

[4]Foster, *The Life with God Bible*, xli–xlv.

[5]Willard, *Hearing God*, 161.

[6]Willard, *Hearing God*, 46.

Notes

FOREWORD

[1] John Ortberg, "Dallas Willard, a Man from Another 'Time Zone,'" *Christianity Today*, July/August 2013.

[2] The reference here is to a phone conversation with Dallas Willard and John Ortberg that was part of the preparation for the conference, Knowing Christ: Celebrating the Teaching of Dallas Willard for Pastors, Ministry Leaders and Christian Educators, that was sponsored by the Martin Institute and Dallas Willard Research Center in Santa Barbara, California, February 21-23, 2013. This conference was held a few short months before Dallas's death.

[3] These words are from correspondence between Dallas Willard and Westmont College president Gayle Beebe. This was a key desire for Dallas Willard concerning the mission of the Martin Institute and Dallas Willard Research Center. Please see the Institute mission statement for more details: www .westmont.edu/about/institutes-and-centers/martin-institute-christianity -culture.

INTRODUCTION: ENCOUNTERING DALLAS WILLARD

[1] "Rethinking your thinking" was a common way Willard defined *repentance*.

[2] Dallas Willard, "Spiritual Formation and Soul Care" (lecture, Denver Seminary, The Hideaway Inn and Conference Center, January 4-8, 2010), https:// conversatio.org/collections/spiritual-formation-and-soul-care-video/.

[3] Dallas Willard, *The Spirit of the Disciplines: Understanding How God Changes Lives* (New York: HarperOne, 1999), 258.

[4] Dallas Willard, *Living in Christ's Presence* (Downers Grove, IL: InterVarsity Press, 2014), 144.

[5]Listen to this quotation in "Introducing Conversatio Divina" (Conversatio Divina, May 8, 2020), www.youtube.com/watch?time_continue=6&v=YU1 b2NmRDZY. The audio from the referenced clip comes from "Living Eternally in the Moment," beginning at 6:10. This can be found on YouTube (www .youtube.com/watch?v=sxKs4rZUqGU&t=3s) or https://dwillard.org/resources /video/living-eternally-in-the-moment-westmont-commencement.

[6]Dallas Willard, "Spirituality and the Churches" (lecture, Fuller Theological Seminary, June 4, 2012), https://conversatio.org/spirituality-and-the -churches/?collection=2409.

[7]Dallas Willard, *Renovation of the Heart: Putting on the Character of Christ* (Colorado Springs: NavPress, 2012), 22.

[8]James Bryan Smith, "Techniques without Transformation," *Christianity Today*, September 2022, 44. Given Smith's intended audience of *Christianity Today* readers, I believe he is indicating that the "modern form" of the spiritual formation movement refers to its expression in the evangelical church. Through God's providence, the spiritual formation movement has an unbroken history. The release of Foster's *Celebration of Discipline* drew wider attention to it primarily, though not exclusively, in the evangelical church.

[9]Willard, *Renovation of the Heart*, chapter 13: "Spiritual Formation in the Local Church."

[10]Willard encouraged churches to make "spiritual formation in Christlikeness the exclusive primary goal of the local congregation." Willard, *Renovation of the Heart*, 235.

[11]Used with permission of Dallas Willard Publications. To hear Dallas pray this prayer, listen to his lecture noted in chapter four, "Spirituality and the Gospel of Christ."

1. SCRIPTURE AS A GATEWAY TO ETERNAL LIVING

[1]Dallas Willard, "Spiritual Formation and Soul Care" (lecture, Denver Seminary, The Hideaway Inn and Conference Center, January 4-8, 2010), https:// conversatio.org/collections/spiritual-formation-and-soul-care-video/.

[2]Dallas Willard, *Living in Christ's Presence* (Downers Grove, IL: InterVarsity Press, 2014), 81.

[3]Since this course, I've also seen Willard describe beauty as "goodness made visible to the senses." Thanks to Becky Willard Heatley for reminding me of this.

[4]Willard, "Spiritual Formation and Soul Care." The class was recorded and the quotes and notes I include here can all be found online in context at https://dwillard.org/resources/video/human-contribution-to-holiness.

[5]John Ortberg, "Dallas Willard, a Man from Another 'Time Zone,'" *Christianity Today*, July/August 2013.

[6]Michael Stewart Robb, *The Kingdom Among Us: The Gospel According to Dallas Willard* (Minneapolis: Fortress Press, 2022), 12.

[7]Dallas Willard, *The Divine Conspiracy: Rediscovering Our Hidden Life with God* (San Francisco: HarperOne, 1997), 62.

[8]Willard, *The Divine Conspiracy*, 63.

[9]Willard, *The Divine Conspiracy*, 63.

[10]Gary Black Jr., *The Theology of Dallas Willard: Discovering Protoevangelical Faith* (Eugene, OR: Pickwick Publications, 2013), 89.

[11]Willard, *The Divine Conspiracy*, 329.

[12]Willard, *The Divine Conspiracy*, 41.

[13]Willard, *The Divine Conspiracy*, 41.

[14]Willard, *The Divine Conspiracy*, 41.

[15]Willard, *The Divine Conspiracy*, 42.

[16]Willard, *The Divine Conspiracy*, 42.

[17]Willard, *The Divine Conspiracy*, 49.

[18]Willard, *The Divine Conspiracy*, 49. Translation by Dallas Willard.

[19]Willard, *The Divine Conspiracy*, 49.

[20]Willard, *The Divine Conspiracy*, 50.

[21]J. P. Moreland, "Reflections on a Day with My Professor and Friend," in *Eternal Living: Reflections on Dallas Willard's Teaching on Faith and Formation*, ed. Gary W. Moon (Downers Grove, IL: InterVarsity Press, 2015), 124.

[22]Moreland, "Reflections," 122.

[23]Moreland, "Reflections," 123.

[24]Moreland, "Reflections," 122.

[25]Moreland, "Reflections," 123.

[26]Dallas Willard, *Hearing God: Developing a Conversational Relationship with God* (Downers Grove, IL: InterVarsity Press, 1999), 161. Excerpts from *Hearing God* used by permission of InterVarsity Press, PO Box 1400, Downers Grove, IL 60515, USA. www.ivpress.com.

2. SOUTHERN BAPTIST, PHILOSOPHER, MYSTIC

[1]Richard Plass and James Cofield, *The Relational Soul: Moving from False Self to Deep Connection* (Downers Grove, IL: InterVarsity Press, 2014), 140-43.

[2]Eugene Peterson, *The Pastor* (New York: HarperOne, 2011), 215.

[3]Gary W. Moon, "Living in the Glow of God," in *Eternal Living: Reflections on Dallas Willard's Teaching on Faith & Formation*, ed. Gary W. Moon (Downers Grove, IL: InterVarsity Press, 2015), 28-29.

[4]For a timeline of Willard's life, visit conversatio.org/about.

[5]Michael Stewart Robb, *The Kingdom Among Us: The Gospel According to Dallas Willard* (Minneapolis: Fortress Press, 2022), 11.

[6]Dallas Willard, *Hearing God: Developing a Conversational Relationship with God* (Downers Grove, IL: InterVarsity Press, 1999), 141.

[7]Willard, *Hearing God*, 141.

[8]Willard, *Hearing God*, 142.

[9]Willard, *Hearing God*, 142.

[10]Willard, *Hearing God*, 142.

[11]Willard, *Hearing God*, 142.

[12]Willard, *Hearing God*, 142-43.

[13]Willard, *Hearing God*, 103.

[14]Gary W. Moon, *Becoming Dallas Willard: The Formation of a Philosopher, Teacher, and Christ Follower* (Downers Grove, IL: InterVarsity Press, 2018), 72.

[15]Dallas Willard, *The Divine Conspiracy: Rediscovering Our Hidden Life with God* (San Francisco: HarperOne, 1997), xvi.

[16]Willard, *The Divine Conspiracy*, xvi.

[17]Dallas Willard, *The Allure of Gentleness* (New York: HarperOne, 2015), 104.

[18]Willard, *The Allure of Gentleness*, 104.

[19]Willard, *The Allure of Gentleness*, 107.

[20]Willard, *The Allure of Gentleness*, 108.

[21]Willard, *The Allure of Gentleness*, 108.

[22]Willard, *The Allure of Gentleness*, 106.

[23]Willard, *The Allure of Gentleness*, 107.

[24]Willard, *The Allure of Gentleness*, 108-9.

[25]J. P. Moreland, "Reflections on a Day with My Professor and Friend," in *Eternal Living: Reflections on Dallas Willard's Teaching on Faith and Formation*, ed. Gary W. Moon (Downers Grove, IL: InterVarsity Press, 2015), 119.

26 Moreland, "Reflections," 121.

27 Moreland, "Reflections," 124. See also Moon, *Becoming Dallas Willard*, 193.

28 Moreland, "Reflections," 125.

29 Moreland, "Reflections," 124.

30 Gary W. Moon, "Willard's Four Critical Commitments: The Essential Quadrilateral for Authentic Spiritual Change and Transformation" (Conversatio Divina, July 15, 2022), https://conversatio.org/willards-four-critical-commitments/.

31 Moreland, "Reflections," 125. See also Moon, *Becoming Dallas Willard*, 193.

32 Moreland, "Reflections," 126.

33 Moon, "Willard's Four Critical Commitments."

34 Moon, "Willard's Four Critical Commitments."

35 Moon, *Becoming Dallas Willard*, 193.

36 Moon, *Becoming Dallas Willard*, 193.

37 Moon, "Willard's Four Critical Commitments."

38 Dallas Willard, *The Spirit of the Disciplines: Understanding How God Changes Lives* (New York: HarperOne, 1999), 69.

39 Willard, *The Spirit of the Disciplines*, 108.

40 Willard, *The Spirit of the Disciplines*, 108.

41 Willard, *The Spirit of the Disciplines*, 109.

42 Willard, *The Spirit of the Disciplines*, 109.

43 Willard, *The Spirit of the Disciplines*, 109-110.

44 Willard, *The Spirit of the Disciplines*, 110.

45 Willard, *The Spirit of the Disciplines*, 110.

46 Willard, *The Spirit of the Disciplines*, 110.

47 Willard, *The Spirit of the Disciplines*, 111.

48 Willard, *The Spirit of the Disciplines*, 111.

49 Robb, *The Kingdom Among Us*, 163. For an in-depth treatment of this philosophical topic, I recommend Walter Hopp's *Phenomenology: A Contemporary Introduction* (New York: Routledge, 2020).

50 Robb, *The Kingdom Among Us*, 501.

51 Willard, *The Divine Conspiracy*, 25.

52 Willard, *The Divine Conspiracy*, 27.

53 Moon, "Living in the Glow of God," 27.

54 Moon, *Becoming Dallas Willard*, 63.

55 Willard, *Hearing God*, 161.

[56]Willard, *Hearing God*, 161.

[57]Willard, *Hearing God*, 56.

[58]Willard, *Hearing God*, 48.

[59]Trevor Hudson, *Seeking God* (Colorado Springs: NavPress, 2022), 1. To study more about Dallas's mystical experiences, I recommend his article, "When God Moves In: My Experience with *Deeper Experiences of Famous Christians*," which is included in *The Great Omission* (New York: HarperOne, 2006).

[60]Dallas Willard, *Renovation of the Heart: Putting on the Character of Christ* (Colorado Springs: NavPress, 2012), 68.

3. GETTING THE BIBLE THROUGH US

[1]*How to Read a Book* by Mortimer Adler was also used by Willard as a recommended textbook in one of his philosophy courses at USC.

[2]My Denver Seminary professor, Dr. Howard Baker, who facilitated the Willard course, reminded me of when Dallas was asked why he chose to read from the NASB translation of Scripture. Willard's reply was succinct and straight to the point: "Because it's the best." Classic Dallas.

[3]But to be clear, like many of my other seminary professors who referenced their own books in class, Dallas marked up these teaching copies of his books to aid his ability to instruct.

[4]Gary W. Moon, *Becoming Dallas Willard: The Formation of a Philosopher, Teacher, and Christ Follower* (Downers Grove, IL: InterVarsity Press, 2018), 175.

[5]Moon, *Becoming Dallas Willard*, 176.

[6]Richard Foster et al., eds., *The Life with God Bible* (New York: Harper Collins, 2005), xv.

[7]Foster, *The Life with God Bible*, xxvii.

[8]Foster, *The Life with God Bible*, 1.

[9]Foster, *The Life with God Bible*, xli-xlvii. This Bible includes a listing of the deuterocanonical books, which I have excluded from this list. Also to note, these books were categorized by their content, not by the date of their composition.

[10]Dallas Willard, *The Spirit of the Disciplines: Understanding How God Changes Lives* (New York: HarperOne, 1999), xii.

[11]Willard, *The Spirit of the Disciplines*, 156.

[12]Willard, *The Spirit of the Disciplines*, 156.

13 Willard, *The Spirit of the Disciplines*, 158.

14 Willard, *The Spirit of the Disciplines*, 176.

15 Willard, *The Spirit of the Disciplines*, 176.

16 Willard, *The Spirit of the Disciplines*, 177.

17 Willard, *The Spirit of the Disciplines*, 177.

18 Dallas Willard, *Life Without Lack: Living in the Fullness of Psalm 23* (Nashville: Thomas Nelson, 2019), xvi.

19 Willard, *The Spirit of the Disciplines*, 150.

20 Dallas Willard, *Hearing God: Developing a Conversational Relationship with God* (Downers Grove, IL: InterVarsity Press, 1999), 161.

21 Dallas Willard, *Renovation of the Heart: Putting on the Character of Christ* (Colorado Springs: NavPress, 2012), 122.

22 Willard, *Hearing God*, 161.

23 Willard, *Hearing God*, 162.

24 Willard, *Hearing God*, 163.

25 To add to this, Dallas often told students in his Fuller Seminary class, Spirituality and Ministry, to read the New Testament three times in a week for the purpose of intensity—a deep immersion into the text. Thanks to Jan Johnson for this additional insight.

26 Dallas Willard, "Becoming the Kind of Leaders Who Can Do the Job," *Cutting Edge* (Summer 1999): 13, https://dwillard.org/resources/articles /becoming-the-kinds-of-leaders-who-can-do-the-job. See also, Dallas Willard, "Rules for Religious Leadership," in *Renewing the Christian Mind*, ed. Gary Black Jr. (New York: HarperOne, 2016).

27 Willard, *Hearing God*, 163.

28 Willard, *Hearing God*, 164.

29 Willard, *Hearing God*, 90.

30 Willard, *Hearing God*, 35.

31 Willard, *Hearing God*, 36.

32 Willard, *Hearing God*, 36.

33 Willard, *Life Without Lack*, xvii.

34 Willard, *Hearing God*, 36.

35 Willard, *Hearing God*, 59.

36 Willard, *Hearing God*, 58.

37 Willard, *Hearing God*, 59.

38 Willard, *Hearing God*, 107.

[39]Richard J. Foster, video call, May 3, 2024. Many thanks to Charles Galda, president of Vision New England, and Ted Harro, president of Renovaré, for hosting this call.

[40]Willard, *Hearing God*, 107.

[41]Dallas Willard, "Study and Meditation" (sermon, Rolling Hills Covenant Church, February 25, 1981), https://conversatio.org/study-and-meditation/.

[42]Willard, "Study and Meditation."

4. READING SCRIPTURE LIKE SAINT IGNATIUS

[1]Dallas Willard, endorsement in Larry Warner, *Journey with Jesus: Discovering the Spiritual Exercises of Saint Ignatius* (Downers Grove, IL: InterVarsity Press, 2010).

[2]Dallas Willard, *The Divine Conspiracy: Rediscovering Our Hidden Life with God* (San Francisco: HarperOne, 1997), xvii.

[3]Kevin O'Brien, SJ, *The Ignatian Adventure: Experiencing the Spiritual Exercises of Saint Ignatius in Daily Life* (Chicago: Loyola Press, 2011), 270.

[4]O'Brien, *Ignatian Adventure*, 5.

[5]Brian Grogan, SJ, *Alone and on Foot: Ignatius of Loyola* (Dublin: Veritas, 2009), 24.

[6]Grogan, *Alone and on Foot*, 29.

[7]Grogan, *Alone and on Foot*, 38.

[8]Trevor Hudson, "Listening to the Life of Ignatius (Part One)" (lecture, Fuller Theological Seminary, September 25, 2019).

[9]Quoted in O'Brien, *Ignatian Adventure*, 8-9.

[10]O'Brien, *Ignatian Adventure*, 14.

[11]David Fleming, SJ, *Draw Me into Your Friendship: The Spiritual Exercises* (Saint Louis, MO: Institute of Jesuit Sources, 1996), 27.

[12]David L. Fleming, SJ, *What Is Ignatian Spirituality?* (Chicago: Loyola Press, 2008), 8.

[13]Willard, *The Divine Conspiracy*, 62.

[14]Willard, *The Divine Conspiracy*, 61-62.

[15]Gerard Manley Hopkins, "As Kingfishers Catch Fire," Poetry Foundation, accessed February 8, 2024, www.poetryfoundation.org/poems/44389/as-kingfishers-catch-fire. For readers familiar with the works of Eugene Peterson, you may recognize that Peterson impressively titled not one, but two of his books from this poem: *Christ Plays in Ten Thousand Places* and *As*

Kingfishers Catch Fire. I call attention to this to note the significant influence Ignatius continues to have on the broader spiritual formation movement today.

[16]To hear Dallas talk about the magnificence of God, listen to his lecture "Spirituality and the Gospel of Christ," (lecture at Fuller Seminary, Pasadena, CA, June 4, 2012), found at https://conversatio.org/spirituality-and-the-gospel-of-christ/?collection=2409.

[17]This trinitarian framework is inspired by Darrell Johnson's *Experiencing the Trinity: Living in the Relationship at the Centre of the Universe* (Vancouver, BC: Canadian Church Leaders Network, 2021), 52.

[18]Quoted in Gary W. Moon, "Willard's Four Critical Commitments: The Essential Quadrilateral for Authentic Spiritual Change and Transformation," (Conversatio Divina, July 15, 2022), https://conversatio.org/willards-four-critical-commitments/.

[19]O'Brien, *Ignatian Adventure*, 95.

[20]Trevor Hudson, *Seeking God* (Colorado Springs: NavPress, 2022), 111.

[21]Hudson, *Seeking God*, 112.

[22]Adapted from Hudson, *Seeking God*, 118-19.

[23]O'Brien, *Ignatian Adventure*, 138.

[24]See Mark 6:31.

[25]O'Brien, *Ignatian Adventure*, 141.

[26]Dallas Willard, *Hearing God: Developing a Conversational Relationship with God* (Downers Grove, IL: InterVarsity Press, 1999), 36.

[27]Hudson, *Seeking God*, 121.

[28]Fleming, *What Is Ignatian Spirituality?*, 19.

[29]Fleming, *What Is Ignatian Spirituality?*, 21.

[30]Fleming, *What Is Ignatian Spirituality?*, 21.

5. THE IMMERSE METHOD

[1]Dallas Willard, "Atonement in the Spiritual Life" (seminar, National Pastors Convention, Youth Specialties, San Diego, March 10, 2004), MP3, 1:06:00. Cited in Michael Stewart Robb, *The Kingdom Among Us: The Gospel According to Dallas Willard* (Minneapolis: Fortress Press, 2022), 59.

[2]Dallas Willard, *Renovation of the Heart: Putting on the Character of Christ* (Colorado Springs: NavPress, 2012), 240.

[3]Dallas Willard, *The Great Omission: Reclaiming Jesus's Essential Teachings on Discipleship* (New York: HarperOne, 2006), 20.

[4]Dallas Willard, *Hearing God: Developing a Conversational Relationship with God* (Downers Grove, IL: InterVarsity Press, 1999), 155.

[5]Willard, *Hearing God*, 161.

[6]Willard, *Hearing God*, 155.

[7]Gary W. Moon, *Falling for God: Saying Yes to His Extravagant Proposal* (New York: WaterBrook Press, 2004), 197.

[8]Moon, *Falling for God*, 197.

[9]Willard, *Hearing God*, 164.

[10]Willard, *Hearing God*, 56.

[11]Willard, *Hearing God*, 141.

[12]Dallas Willard, *The Allure of Gentleness: Defending the Faith in the Manner of Jesus* (New York: HarperOne, 2015), 107.

[13]Willard, *Hearing God*, 89, 1 Kings 19:12 KJV.

[14]Willard, *Hearing God*, 163.

[15]Willard, *Hearing God*, 90.

[16]Willard, *Hearing God*, 91.

[17]Willard, *Hearing God*, 184.

[18]Willard, *Hearing God*, 162.

[19]Madame Guyon, *Experiencing the Depth of Jesus Christ* (Goleta, CA: Christian Books, 1975), 16, cited in Willard, *Hearing God*, 162-63.

[20]Willard, *Hearing God*, 162.

[21]Willard, *Hearing God*, 161.

[22]Willard, *Hearing God*, 161.

[23]Dallas Willard, *The Spirit of the Disciplines: Understanding How God Changes Lives* (New York: HarperOne, 1999), 177.

[24]Willard, *The Spirit of the Disciplines*, 177.

[25]Dallas Willard, *Life Without Lack: Living in the Fullness of Psalm 23* (Nashville: Thomas Nelson, 2019), 2.

[26]Willard, *The Great Omission*, 58.

[27]Steve L. Porter, "The Evidential Force of Dallas Willard," in *Eternal Living: Reflections on Dallas Willard's Teaching on Faith & Formation*, ed. Gary W. Moon (Downers Grove, IL: InterVarsity Press, 2015), 88.

[28]Willard, *Life Without Lack*, xvi.

[29]Porter, "The Evidential Force of Dallas Willard," 88.

[30]Willard, *Hearing God*, 155.

[31]David L. Fleming, SJ, *What Is Ignatian Spirituality?* (Chicago: Loyola Press, 2008), 92.

[32] Dallas Willard, *The Divine Conspiracy: Rediscovering Our Hidden Life with God* (San Francisco: HarperOne, 1997), 352.

[33] Gary W. Moon, *Becoming Dallas Willard: The Formation of a Philosopher, Teacher, and Christ Follower* (Downers Grove, IL: InterVarsity Press, 2018), 195.

[34] Moon, *Becoming Dallas Willard*, 193.

[35] Moon, *Becoming Dallas Willard*, 195.

[36] Gary Moon, *Apprenticeship with Jesus: Learning to Live Like the Master* (Grand Rapids, MI: Baker, 2009), 241.

[37] If you've seen the Disney movie *Frozen 2*, you know Dallas Willard was likely unintentionally plagiarized. The movie's key line is "Do the next right thing."

[38] Dallas Willard, "Your Place in This World," in *Renewing the Christian Mind*, ed. Gary Black Jr. (New York: HarperOne, 2016), 241.

[39] Willard, *Hearing God*, 164.

[40] Willard, *Hearing God*, 36.

[41] Willard, *The Divine Conspiracy*, 241.

[42] Willard, *The Divine Conspiracy*, 242.

[43] Willard, *Hearing God*, 161.

[44] Willard, *The Spirit of the Disciplines*, 173.

[45] Robb, *The Kingdom Among Us*, 163.

[46] Trevor Hudson, *Seeking God* (Colorado Springs: NavPress, 2022), 10.

[47] Dallas Willard, "Live Life to the Full," *Christian Herald* (UK), April 14, 2001, https://dwillard.org/articles/live-life-to-the-full.

[48] Willard, *The Spirit of the Disciplines*, 10.

6. EXPERIENCING THE OLD TESTAMENT

[1] Dallas Willard, *The Divine Conspiracy: Rediscovering Our Hidden Life with God* (San Francisco: HarperOne, 1997), 329.

[2] Michael Ramsey, quoted in Trevor Hudson, *Discovering Our Spiritual Identity* (Downers Grove: InterVarsity Press, 2010), 16.

[3] Michael Stewart Robb, *The Kingdom Among Us: The Gospel According to Dallas Willard* (Minneapolis: Fortress Press, 2022), 30.

[4] Robb, *The Kingdom Among Us*, 36.

[5] Robb, *The Kingdom Among Us*, 44.

[6] Robb, *The Kingdom Among Us*, 45. To clarify further, Robb summarizes the historical view of progressive revelation as "the theory that God guards but gradually lets out important information about himself over time."

[7]Robb, *The Kingdom Among Us*, 45.

[8]This talk is referenced in Robb, *The Kingdom Among Us*, 46, as Dallas Willard, "Does God Talk to Girls?," *A Woman's Prerogative in Christ* (Valley Vista Christian Community, Sepulveda, CA, November 1987), MP3/cassette, 1:11:00. This collection of teachings can be accessed at https://conversatio .org/collections/a-womans-prerogative-in-christ-womens-retreat/. This quotation is stated at 1:13:48 in the lecture.

[9]For more of Willard's commentary on Achan's sin, see Dallas Willard, *The Allure of Gentleness* (New York: HarperOne, 2015), 103. To briefly summarize, because Achan had taken some of the "devoted things" from Jericho he was forbidden from taking, his entire family was stoned to death and then burned with all their belongings. Dallas comments, "Since we read about this in the Bible, we automatically assume that this is a punishment dictated by God. But this was a cultural norm at that time throughout the known world."

[10]Richard Foster et al., eds., *The Life with God Bible* (New York: Harper Collins, 2005), xxvi–xxvii. For more on progressive apprehension, check out Dallas Willard Ministries' School of Kingdom Living. As part of the course curriculum, faculty member, Keith Matthews—a long-time colleague and friend of Willard's—teaches the principles of progressive apprehension. Keith shared this with me over a Zoom call on July 29, 2024.

[11]Dallas Willard, *The Spirit of the Disciplines: Understanding How God Changes Lives* (New York: HarperOne, 1999), 62.

[12]Willard, *The Spirit of the Disciplines*, 63.

[13]Willard, *The Spirit of the Disciplines*, 63.

[14]Robb, *The Kingdom Among Us*, 416.

[15]Willard, *The Spirit of the Disciplines*, 63.

[16]Robb, *The Kingdom Among Us*, 424.

[17]Robb, *The Kingdom Among Us*, 424.

[18]Willard's quotations and commentary on Numbers 6 can all be found in Dallas Willard, *Living in Christ's Presence* (Downers Grove, IL: InterVarsity Press, 2014), 164–67.

[19]Dallas Willard, *The Great Omission: Reclaiming Jesus's Essential Teachings on Discipleship* (New York: HarperOne, 2006), 58–59.

[20]Dallas Willard, *Life Without Lack: Living in the Fullness of Psalm 23* (Nashville: Thomas Nelson, 2019), xvii–xx.

[21]Dallas Willard, *Hearing God: Developing a Conversational Relationship with God* (Downers Grove, IL: InterVarsity Press, 1999), 18.

[22]Willard, *Hearing God*, 11.

7. EXPERIENCING THE NEW TESTAMENT

[1]Dallas Willard, *The Divine Conspiracy: Rediscovering Our Hidden Life with God* (San Francisco: HarperOne, 1997), 95.

[2]Dallas Willard, *Knowing Christ Today: Why We Can Trust Spiritual Knowledge* (New York: HarperOne, 2009), 45.

[3]Willard, *Knowing Christ Today*, 50.

[4]Willard, *Knowing Christ Today*, 46.

[5]Willard, *Knowing Christ Today*, 52.

[6]Willard, *Knowing Christ Today*, 47.

[7]Willard, *Knowing Christ Today*, 53.

[8]Willard, *Knowing Christ Today*, 48.

[9]Willard, *Knowing Christ Today*, 53.

[10]Willard's interpretation of the Beatitudes is elucidated in chapter 4 of *The Divine Conspiracy*, "Who Is Really Well Off?—The Beatitudes."

[11]Willard, *The Divine Conspiracy*, 106.

[12]Willard, *The Divine Conspiracy*, 97.

[13]Willard, *The Divine Conspiracy*, 102.

[14]Gregg Ten Elshof, "Neither Because nor In Spite Of: A Critical Reflection on Willard's Read of the Beatitudes," in *Until Christ Is Formed in You: Dallas Willard and Spiritual Formation*, eds. Steven L. Porter, Gary W. Moon, and J. P. Moreland (Abilene, TX: Abilene Christian University Press, 2018), 81.

[15]Ten Elshof, "Neither Because nor In Spite Of," 83.

[16]Ten Elshof, "Neither Because nor In Spite Of," 84.

[17]Ten Elshof, "Neither Because nor In Spite Of," 86.

[18]Willard, *The Divine Conspiracy*, 268.

[19]Willard, *The Divine Conspiracy*, 269.

[20]Willard, *The Divine Conspiracy*, 269.

[21]Willard, *The Divine Conspiracy*, 269.

[22]For more on why Willard would translate *heaven* as "always near us," see his extended discussion on "The Heavens as the Human Environment" in *The Divine Conspiracy*, 66–74.

[23]Willard, *The Divine Conspiracy*, 66.

[24]Willard, *The Divine Conspiracy*, 66–67.

[25]Willard, *Knowing Christ Today*, 53.

[26]Dallas Willard, *Renovation of the Heart: Putting on the Character of Christ* (Colorado Springs: NavPress, 2012), 55.

[27]Willard, *Renovation of the Heart*, 56.

[28]Dallas Willard, *Life Without Lack: Living in the Fullness of Psalm 23* (Nashville: Thomas Nelson, 2019), 95.

[29]Willard, *Renovation of the Heart*, 129.

8. TEACHING SCRIPTURE LIKE DALLAS WILLARD

[1]Dallas Willard, *Knowing Christ Today: Why We Can Trust Spiritual Knowledge* (New York: HarperOne, 2009), 193.

[2]Dallas Willard, "A Cup Running Over," in *The Art & Craft of Biblical Preaching*, eds. Haddon Robinson and Craig Brian Larson (Grand Rapids, MI: Zondervan, 2005), 71.

[3]Willard, "A Cup Running Over," 73.

[4]Dallas Willard, *Life Without Lack: Living in the Fullness of Psalm 23* (Nashville: Thomas Nelson, 2019), 124.

[5]Dallas Willard, "Becoming the Kind of Leaders Who Can Do the Job," *Cutting Edge* (Summer 1999): 14.

[6]Jan Johnson, "A Word from a Different Reality," in *Eternal Living: Reflections on Dallas Willard's Teaching on Faith & Formation*, ed. Gary W. Moon (Downers Grove, IL: InterVarsity Press, 2015), 67.

[7]Dallas Willard, *Renovation of the Heart: Putting on the Character of Christ* (Colorado Springs: NavPress, 2012), 246-47.

[8]Willard, "Becoming the Kind of Leaders Who Can Do the Job," 13.

[9]Willard, "Becoming the Kind of Leaders Who Can Do the Job," 15.

[10]Dallas Willard, *The Divine Conspiracy: Rediscovering Our Hidden Life with God* (San Francisco: HarperOne, 1997), 114.

[11]Gary W. Moon, "Dallas Willard's First Concern: Robust Metaphysical Realism and the Kingdom of God—Here and Now" (lecture, Fuller Theological Seminary, Malibu, CA, October 1, 2019).

[12]For an introduction to this concept, see *Knowing Christ Today*, chapter three: "How Moral Knowledge Disappeared."

[13]Willard, *Knowing Christ Today*, 72.

[14]To explore this theme in greater depth, see the posthumously released, Dallas Willard, *The Disappearance of Moral Knowledge* (New York: Routledge

University Press, 2018), edited by three of Dallas's PhD students, Steven L. Porter, Aaron Preston and Gregg A. Ten Elshof.

[15] Willard, "Becoming the Kind of Leaders Who Can Do the Job," 15.

[16] Willard, "A Cup Running Over," 73.

[17] Willard, "Becoming the Kind of Leaders Who Can Do the Job," 15.

[18] Larissa Heatley, "Family Voices," in *Eternal Living*, 58-59.

[19] Willard, *Renovation of the Heart*, 85.

[20] Dallas Willard, "How to Love Your Neighbor as Yourself," in *Renewing the Christian Mind*, ed. Gary Black Jr. (New York: HarperOne, 2016), 129.

[21] Willard, "How to Love Your Neighbor," 131.

[22] Willard, "How to Love Your Neighbor," 131.

[23] Willard, "How to Love Your Neighbor," 131.

[24] Willard, "How to Love Your Neighbor," 134.

[25] According to the Willard family, Dallas desired to be in intensive educational settings with students over the course of several days. He preferred for students to have completed reading assignments ahead of time and enjoyed getting to listen to students' stories one-on-one over meals, as he did with me. His hope was for the people he taught to go and share with others in their spheres of influence what they experienced.

[26] For more on Willard's relationship with *Celebration of Discipline* author Richard Foster, see Gary W. Moon's biography *Becoming Dallas Willard* (Downers Grove, IL: InterVarsity Press, 2018).

[27] Willard, *The Divine Conspiracy*, 58.

[28] Willard, "Becoming the Kind of Leaders Who Can Do the Job," 14.

[29] Willard, *Renovation of the Heart*, 209.

[30] Willard, *Renovation of the Heart*, 210.

[31] Willard, "A Cup Running Over," 71-72.

[32] Dallas Willard, "My Journey to and Beyond Tenure in a Secular University" (address, C. S. Lewis Foundation Summer Conference, San Diego, June 21, 2003), https://dwillard.org/resources/articles/my-journey-to-and-beyond -tenure-in-a-secular-university.

[33] Dallas Willard, "Your Place in This World," in *Renewing the Christian Mind*, ed. Gary Black Jr. (New York: HarperOne, 2016), 244.

[34] Dallas Willard, "Life in the Spirit" (chapel address, Wheaton College, Wheaton, IL, April 17, 2009), www.youtube.com/watch?v=60kOaLMU FQQ.

CONCLUSION: WE'LL SEE

[1]Dallas Willard, foreword to Gary W. Moon, *Falling for God: Saying Yes to His Extravagant Proposal* (New York: WaterBrook Press, 2004), ix.

[2]Dallas Willard, Renovaré Institute: Denver Cohort, October 12-15, 2010, and March 15-18, 2011, https://conversatio.org/collections/renovare -institute-denver-cohort/.

[3]Dallas Willard, "Spirituality and Ministry" (lecture, Fuller Theological Seminary DMin Cohort, June 4-15, 2012), https://conversatio.org/collections /spirituality-and-ministry-2012/.

[4]Dallas Willard, Recommended Reading, Dallas Willard Ministries, accessed August 3, 2024, https://dwillard.org/resources/recommended-reading.

Also by the Author

The Fellowship of the Suffering
978-8038-4530-9

Like this book?

Scan the code to discover more content like this!

Get on IVP's email list to receive special offers, exclusive book news, and thoughtful content from your favorite authors on topics you care about.

 InterVarsity Press